War—
Patriotism—
Peace

By LEO TOLSTOI

Edited, with Introduction, by
SCOTT NEARING

NEW YORK
VANGUARD PRESS

FOREWORD

TOLSTOI AS AN ANTI-WAR AGITATOR

MANY voices were raised against war during those recent years when the preparations for war were so widespread, and so threatening to peace and human happiness. Among these voices none sounded more clearly and none was more vigorous than that of Leo Tolstoi.

Tolstoi was a member of the Russian ruling class. His parents were landed aristocrats. He grew up surrounded by the ease, luxury, frivolity and dissipation that were taken for granted by people in his social position. Like many other Russian gentlemen he entered the army, assisted in the siege of Silistri and took part in the defense of Sebastopol in 1854. Tolstoi was then 26 years old.

Military life made a deep impression on Tolstoi's mind. The routine and coercion, as well as the sheer brutality of military activities offended and outraged him. While he was thrilled by the dramatic qualities of war, as pictured in his "Tales from Sebastopol," he was fiercely resentful of its inhumanities.

This resentment grew as Tolstoi became more familiar with the forces operating behind the war-making machine. Time after time he laid aside his other work to pen some letter or some protest or to write some article or essay condemning war, and so effective were his efforts that toward the end of his life (he died in 1910) Tolstoi was looked upon as one of the world's outstanding agitators against war.

Tolstoi spent his mature years in a Europe that was arming and preparing for the War of 1914. He foresaw the war; predicted it; and spent much time and energy trying to create anti-war public opinion.

iii

His propaganda against war was far more than an emotional opposition to mass-murder. Tolstoi felt that opposition, of course. He had been a soldier. He had seen war and had taken part in it. His great novel, "War and Peace," tells how atrocious war really is.

But Tolstoi understood that war was not an accident. He recognized it as a logical product of competition and exploitation. Behind the whole system of landlordism and capitalism, he saw violence and armed force. It was to this cause that he traced war, and it was against this exploitation and this violence that he hurled his denunciations.

"The ownership of the land," he writes in "Need it Be So?" "having originated in violence (through conquest people appropriated the land, and then gave it away and sold it), has remained, in spite of every effort at turning it into a right, nothing but an act of violence of the strong and armed against the weak and unarmed."

Having secured the land by force, the rich "gather in one place and settle near other rich people, where the gratification of all kinds of luxurious tastes is cautiously guarded by a numerous police force." ("What Shall We Do Then?" Ch. 13.) When the poor resent this appropriation of the good things of life by the rich, they are jailed or executed for the protection of property and of property rights. Under such a system, "there will always be wars for markets, for gold fields, and so forth, which we need in order to maintain our exclusive wealth." ("Who is to Blame?")

Thus the police and the army become the tools of the rich and powerful, to protect their riches and power against the poor, and to help them add more riches and power to those they already possess. The source of the war motive thus lies in the economic struggle between men.

But the actual propaganda in favor of war takes the form of an appeal to patriotism. In the name of religion; in the name of their national traditions; in the names of their ancestors; in the name of justice and liberty, the workers and farmers of one country are urged to "protect" themselves against the workers and farmers of other countries. Thus patriotism becomes one of the leading instruments for the making of wars. Therefore Tolstoi appeals, not only to the soldiers and officers, in his efforts to create sentiment against war. He also directs his attack against the whole system of nationalism out of which wars grow.

Finally, he insists that men must refuse to do violence, whether as soldiers or magistrates or as citizens. Only then will violence be abolished. Only then will intelligence reign. Only then can we build "a free and loving union of men."

Tolstoi is dead. Wars go on.

The World War was not the last war—it was the First World War. The causes which brought it about are still operating. The preparations for the Second World War are now being made by all the great powers, and unless some miracle intervenes, the Second World War will take place in the not distant future. And when it does occur it will be far more terrible than the First World War, because the weapons of destruction are far more numerous and efficient today than they were in 1914.

This is a time when every man and woman who is against mass-murder should bend his efforts to the task of removing the causes of war. After the war begins, it is already too late.

Tolstoi presents one powerful line of argument against war. This argument should be studied and understood. The essays and letters printed in this volume furnish an invaluable fund of information and provide a real insight into the causes that are driving the world toward another ghastly orgy of blood-letting.

SCOTT NEARING.

CONTENTS

WAR—PATRIOTISM—PEACE

NEGLECT THE FIRE AND YOU CANNOT PUT IT OUT

(1885)

THERE lived in a village a peasant, by the name of Iván Shcherbakóv. He lived well; he was himself in full strength, the first worker in the village, and he had three sons,—all of them on their legs: one was married, the second about to marry, and the third a grown-up lad who drove horses and was beginning to plough. Iván's wife was a clever woman and a good housekeeper, and his daughter-in-law turned out to be a quiet person and a good worker. There was no reason why Iván should not have led a good life with his family. The only idle mouth on the farm was his old, ailing father (he had been lying on the oven for seven years, sick with the asthma).

Iván had plenty of everything, three horses and a colt, a cow and a yearling calf, and fifteen sheep. The women made the shoes and the clothes for the men and worked in the field; the men worked on their farms.

They had enough grain until the next crop. From the oats they paid their taxes and met all their obligations. An easy life, indeed, might Iván have led with his children. But next door to him he had a neighbour, Gavrílo the Lame, Gordyéy Ivánov's son. And there was an enmity between him and Iván.

So long as old man Gordyéy was alive, and Iván's father ran

the farm, the peasants lived in neighbourly fashion. If the women needed a sieve or a vat, or the men had to get another axle or wheel for a time, they sent from one farm to another, and helped each other out in a neighbourly way. If a calf ran into the yard of the threshing-floor, they drove it out and only said: "Don't let it out, for the heap has not yet been put away." And it was not their custom to put it away and lock it up in the threshing-floor or in a shed, or to revile each other.

Thus they lived so long as the old men were alive. But when the young people began to farm, things went quite differently.

The whole thing began from a mere nothing. A hen of Iván's daughter-in-law started laying early. The young woman gathered the eggs for Passion week. Every day she went to the shed to pick up an egg from the wagon-box. But, it seems, the boys scared away the hen, and she flew across the wicker fence to the neighbour's yard, and laid an egg there. The young woman heard the hen cackle, so she thought:

"I have no time now, I must get the hut in order for the holiday; I will go there later to get it."

In the evening she went to the wagon-box under the shed, to fetch the egg, but it was not there. The young woman asked her mother-in-law and her brother-in-law if they had taken it; but Taráska, her youngest brother-in-law, said:

"Your hen laid an egg in the neighbour's yard, for she cackled there and flew out from that yard."

The young woman went to look at her hen, and found her sitting with the cock on the perch; she had closed her eyes and was getting ready to sleep. The woman would have liked to ask her where she laid the egg, but she would not have given her any answer. Then the young woman went to her neighbour. The old woman met her.

"What do you want, young woman?"

"Granny, my hen has been in your yard to-day,—did she not lay an egg there?"

"I have not set eyes on her. We have hens of our own,

thank God, and they have been laying for quite awhile. We have gathered our own eggs, and we do not need other people's eggs. Young woman, we do not go to other people's yards to gather eggs."

The young woman was offended. She said a word too much, the neighbour answered with two, and the women began to scold. Iván's wife was carrying water, and she, too, took a hand in it. Gavrílo's wife jumped out, and began to rebuke her neighbour. She reminded her of things that had happened, and mentioned things that had not happened at all. And the tongue-lashing began. All yelled together, trying to say two words at the same time. And they used bad words.

"You are such and such a one; you are a thief, a sneak; you are simply starving your father-in-law; you are a tramp."

"And you are a beggar: you have torn my sieve; and you have our shoulder-yoke. Give me back the yoke!"

They grabbed the yoke, spilled the water, tore off their kerchiefs, and began to fight. Gavrílo drove up from the field, and he took his wife's part. Iván jumped out with his son, and they all fell in a heap. Iván was a sturdy peasant, and he scattered them all. He yanked out a piece of Gavrílo's beard. People ran up to them, and they were with difficulty pulled apart.

That's the way it began.

Gavrílo wrapped the piece of his beard in a petition and went to the township court to enter a complaint.

"I did not raise a beard for freckled Iván to pull it out."

In the meantime his wife bragged to the neighbours that they would now get Iván sentenced and would have him sent to Siberia, and the feud began.

The old man on the oven tried to persuade them to stop the first day they started to quarrel, but the young people paid no attention to him. He said to them:

"Children, you are doing a foolish thing, and for a foolish thing have you started a feud. Think of it,—the whole affair began from an egg. The children picked up the egg,—well, God be with them! There is no profit in one egg. With God's aid there will be enough for everybody. Well, you have said a bad word, so correct it, show how to use better words! Well, you have had a fight,—you are sinful people. That, too, happens. Well, go and make peace, and let there be an end to it! If you keep it up, it will only be worse."

The young people did not obey the old man; they thought that he was not using sense, but just babbling in old man's fashion.

Iván did not give in to his neighbour.

"I did not pull his beard," he said. "He jerked it out himself; but his son has yanked off my shirt-button and has torn my whole shirt. Here it is."

And Iván, too, took the matter to court. The case was heard before a justice of the peace, and in the township court. While they were suing each other, Gavrílo lost a coupling-pin out of his cart. The women in Gavrílo's house accused Iván's son of having taken it.

"We saw him in the night," they said, "making his way under the window to the cart, and the gossip says that he went to the dram-shop and asked the dram-shopkeeper to take the pin from him."

Again they started a suit. But at home not a day passed but that they quarrelled, nay, even fought. The children cursed one another,—they learned this from their elders,—and when the women met at the brook, they did not so much strike the beetles as let loose their tongues, and to no good.

At first the men just accused each other, but later they began to snatch up things that lay about loose. And they taught the women and children to do the same. Their life grew worse and worse. Iván Shcherbakóv and Gavrílo the Lame kept suing one another at the meetings of the Commune, and in the township court, and before the justices of the peace, and all the judges were tired of them. Now Gavrílo got Iván to pay a fine, or he sent him to the lockup, and now Iván did the same to Gavrílo. And the more they did each other harm, the more furious they grew. When dogs make for each other, they get more enraged the more they fight. You strike a dog from behind, and he thinks that the other dog is biting him, and gets only madder than ever. Just so it was with these peasants: when they went to court, one or the other was punished, either by being made to pay a fine, or by being thrown into prison, and that only made their rage flame up more and more toward one another.

"Just wait, I will pay you back for it!"

And thus it went on for six years. The old man on the oven kept repeating the same advice. He would say to them:

"What are you doing, my children? Drop all your accounts, stick to your work, don't show such malice toward others, and it will be better. The more you rage, the worse will it be."

They paid no attention to the old man.

In the seventh year the matter went so far that Iván's daughter-in-law at a wedding accused Gavrílo before people of having been caught with horses. Gavrílo was drunk, and he did not hold back his anger, but struck the woman and hurt her so that she lay sick for a week, for she was heavy with child. Iván rejoiced, and went with a petition to the prosecuting magistrate.

"Now," he thought, "I will get even with my neighbour: he shall not escape the penitentiary or Siberia."

Again Iván was not successful. The magistrate did not accept the petition: they examined the woman, but she was up and there were no marks upon her. Iván went to the justice of the peace; but the justice sent the case to the township court. Iván bestirred himself in the township office, filled the elder and the scribe with half a bucket of sweet liquor, and got them to sentence Gavrílo to having his back flogged. The sentence was read to Gavrílo in the court.

The scribe read:

"The court has decreed that the peasant Gavrílo Gordyéy receive twenty blows with rods in the township office."

Iván listened to the decree and looked at Gavrílo, wondering what he would do. Gavrílo, too, heard the decree, and he became as pale as a sheet, and turned away and walked out into the vestibule. Iván followed him out and wanted to go to his horse, when he heard Gavrílo say:

"Very well, he will beat my back, and it will burn, but something of his may burn worse than that."

When Iván heard these words, he returned to the judges.

"Righteous judges! He threatens to set fire to my house. Listen, he said it in the presence of witnesses."

Gavrílo was called in.

"Is it true that you said so?"

"I said nothing. Flog me, if you please. Evidently I must suffer for my truth, while he may do anything he wishes."

Gavrílo wanted to say something more, but his lips and cheeks trembled. He turned away toward the wall. Even the judges were frightened as they looked at him.

"It would not be surprising," they thought, "if he actually did some harm to his neighbour or to himself."

And an old judge said to them:

"Listen, friends! You had better make peace with each other. Did you do right, brother Gavrílo, to strike a pregnant woman? Luckily God was merciful to you, but think what crime you might have committed! Is that good? Confess your guilt and beg his pardon. And he will pardon you. Then we shall change the decree."

The scribe heard that, and said:

"That is impossible, because on the basis of Article 117 there has taken place no reconciliation, but the decree of the court has been handed down, and the decree has to be executed."

But the judge paid no attention to the scribe.

"Stop currycombing your tongue. The first article, my friend, is to remember God, and God has commanded me to make peace."

And the judge began once more to talk to the peasants, but he could not persuade them. Gavrílo would not listen to him.

"I am fifty years old less one," he said, "and I have a married son. I have not been beaten in all my life, and now freckled Iván has brought me to being beaten with rods, and am I to beg his forgiveness? Well, he will—Iván will re-member me!"

Gavrílo's voice trembled again. He could not talk. He turned around and went out.

From the township office to the village was a distance of ten versts, and Iván returned home late. The women had already gone out to meet the cattle. He unhitched his horse, put it away, and entered the hut. The room was empty. The children had not yet returned from the field, and the women were out to meet the cattle. Iván went in, sat down on a bench, and began to think. He recalled how the decision was announced to Gavrílo, and how he grew pale, and turned to the wall. And his heart was pinched. He thought of how he should feel if he were condemned to be flogged. He felt sorry for Gavrílo. He heard the old man coughing on the oven. The old man turned around, let down his legs, and sat up. He pulled himself with difficulty up to the bench, and coughed and coughed, until he cleared his throat, and leaned against the table, and said:

"Well, have they condemned him?"

Iván said:

"He has been sentenced to twenty strokes with the rods."

The old man shook his head.

"Iván, you are not doing right. It's wrong, not wrong to him, but to yourself. Well, will it make you feel easier, if they flog him?"

"He will never do it again," said Iván.

"Why not? In what way is he doing worse than you?"

"What, he has not harmed me?" exclaimed Iván. "He might have killed the woman; and he even now threatens to set fire to my house. Well, shall I bow to him for it?"

The old man heaved a sigh, and said:

"You, Iván, walk and drive wherever you please in the free world, and I have passed many years on the oven, and so you think that you see everything, while I see nothing. No, my son, you see nothing,—malice has dimmed your eyes. Another man's sins are in front of you, but your own are behind your back. You say that he has done wrong. If he alone had done wrong, there would be no harm. Does evil between people arise from one man only? Evil arises between two. You see his badness, but you do not see your own. If he himself were bad, and you good, there would be no evil. Who pulled out his beard? Who blasted the rick which was at halves? Who is dragging him to the courts? And yet you put it always on him. You yourself live badly, that's why it is bad. Not thus did I live, and no such thing, my dear, did I teach you. Did I and the old man, his father, live this way? How did we live? In neighbourly fashion. If his flour gave out, and the woman came: 'Uncle Frol, I need some flour.'—'Go, young woman, into the granary, and take as much as you need.' If he had nobody to send out with the horses,—'Go, Iván, and look after his horses!' And if I was short of anything, I used to go to him. 'Uncle Gordyéy, I need this and that.' And how is it now? The other day a soldier was talking about Plévna. Why, your war is worse than what they did at Plévna. Do you call this living? It is a sin! You are a peasant, a head of a house. You will be responsible. What are you teaching your women and your children? To curse. The other day Taráska, that dirty nose, cursed Aunt Arína, and his mother only laughed at him. Is that good? You will be responsible for it. Think of your soul. Is that right? You say a word to me, and I answer with two; you box my ears, and I box you twice. No, my son, Christ walked over the earth and taught us fools something quite different. If a word is said to you,—keep quiet, and let conscience smite him. That's what he, my son, has taught us. If they box your ears, you turn the other cheek to them: 'Here, strike it if I deserve it.' His own conscience will prick him. He will be pacified and will do as you wish. That's what he has commanded us to do, and not to crow. Why are you silent? Do I tell you right?"

Iván was silent, and he listened.

The old man coughed again, and with difficulty coughed up the phlegm, and began to speak again:

"Do you think Christ has taught us anything bad? He has taught us for our own good. Think of your earthly life: are you better off, or worse, since that Plévna of yours was started? Figure out how much you have spent on these courts, how much you have spent in travelling and in feeding yourself on the way? See what eagles of sons you have! You ought to live and live well, and go up, but your property is growing less. Why? For the same reason. From your pride. You ought to be ploughing with the boys in the field and attend to your sowing, but the fiend carries you to court or to some pettifogger. You do not plough in time and do not sow in time, and mother earth does not bring forth anything. Why did the oats not do well this year? When did you sow them? When you came back from the city. And what did you gain from the court? Only trouble for yourself. Oh, son, stick to your business, and attend to your field and your house, and if any one has offended you, forgive him in godly fashion, and things will go better with you, and you will feel easier at heart."

Iván kept silence.

"Listen, Iván! Pay attention to me, an old man. Go and hitch the gray horse, and drive straight back to the office: squash there the whole business, and in the morning go to Gavrílo, make peace with him in godly fashion, and invite him to the holiday" (it was before Lady-day), "have the samovár prepared, get a half bottle, and make an end to all sins, so that they may never happen again, and command the women and children to live in peace."

Iván heaved a sigh, and thought: "The old man is speaking the truth," and his heart melted. The only thing he did not know was how to manage things so as to make peace with his neighbour.

And the old man, as though guessing what he had in mind, began once more:

"Go, Iván, do not put it off! Put out the fire at the start, for when it burns up, you can't control it."

The old man wanted to say something else, but did not

finish, for the women entered the room and began to prattle like magpies. The news had already reached them about how Gavrílo had been sentenced to be flogged, and how he had threatened to set fire to the house. They had found out everything, and had had time in the pasture to exchange words with the women of Gavrílo's house. They said that Gavrílo's daughter-in-law had threatened them with the examining magistrate. The magistrate, they said, was receiving gifts from Gavrílo. He would now upset the whole case, and the teacher had already written another petition to the Tsar about Iván, and that petition mentioned all the affairs, about the coupling-pin, and about the garden,—and half of the estate would go back to him. Iván listened to their talk, and his heart was chilled again, and he changed his mind about making peace with Gavrílo.

In a farmer's yard there is always much to do. Iván did not stop to talk with the women, but got up and went out of the house, and walked over to the threshing-floor and the shed. Before he fixed everything and started back again, the sun went down, and the boys returned from the field. They had been ploughing up the field for the winter crop. Iván met them, and asked them about their work and helped them to put up the horses. He laid aside the torn collar and was about to put some poles under the shed, when it grew quite dark. Iván left the poles until the morrow; instead he threw some fodder down to the cattle, opened the gate, let Taráska out with the horses into the street, to go to the right pasture, and again closed the gate and put down the gate board.

"Now to supper and to bed," thought Iván. He took the torn collar and went into the house. He had entirely forgotten about Gavrílo, and about what his father had told him. As he took hold of the ring and was about to enter the vestibule, he heard his neighbour on the other side of the wicker fence scolding some one in a hoarse voice.

"The devil take him!" Gavrílo was crying to some one. "He ought to be killed."

These words made all the old anger toward his neighbour burst forth in Iván. He stood awhile and listened to Gavrílo's scolding. Then Gavrílo grew quiet, and Iván went into the house.

He entered the room. Fire was burning within. The young woman was sitting in the corner behind the spinning-wheel; the old woman was getting supper ready; the eldest son was making laces for the bast shoes, the second was at the table with a book, and Taráska was getting ready to go to the night pasture.

In the house everything was good and merry, if it were not for that curse,—a bad neighbour.

Iván was angry when he entered the room. He knocked the cat down from the bench and scolded the women because the vat was not in the right place. Iván felt out of humour. He sat down, frowning, and began to mend the collar. He could not forget Gavrílo's words, with which he had threatened him in court, and how he had said about somebody, speaking in a hoarse voice: "He ought to be killed."

The old woman got Taráska something to eat. When he was through with his supper, he put on a fur coat and a caftan, girded himself, took a piece of bread, and went out to the horses. The eldest brother wanted to see him off, but Iván himself got up and went out on the porch. It was pitch-dark outside, the sky was clouded, and a wind had risen. Iván stepped down from the porch, helped his little son to get on a horse, frightened a colt behind him, and stood looking and listening while Taráska rode down the village, where he met other children, and until they all rode out of hearing. Iván stood and stood at the gate, and could not get Gavrílo's words out of his head, "Something of yours may burn worse."

"He will not consider himself," thought Iván. "It is dry, and a wind is blowing. He will enter somewhere from behind, the scoundrel, and will set the house on fire, and he will go free. If I could catch him, he would not get away from me."

This thought troubled Iván so much that he did not go back to the porch, but walked straight into the street and through the gate, around the corner of the house.

"I will examine the yard,—who knows?"

And Iván walked softly down along the gate. He had just turned around the corner and looked up the fence, when it seemed to him that something stirred at the other end, as though it got up and sat down again. Iván stopped and stood still,—he listened and looked: everything was quiet, only the wind rustled the leaves in the willow-tree and crackled through the straw. It was pitch-dark, but his eyes got used to the darkness: Iván could see the whole corner and the plough and the penthouse. He stood and looked, but there was no one there.

"It must have only seemed so to me," thought Iván, "but I will, nevertheless, go and see," and he stole up along the shed. Iván stepped softly in his bast shoes, so that he did not hear his own steps. He came to the corner, when, behold, something flashed by near the plough, and disappeared again. Iván felt as though something hit him in the heart, and he stopped. As he stopped he could see something flashing up, and he could see clearly some one in a cap squatting down with his back toward him, and setting fire to a bunch of straw in his hands. He stood stock-still.

"Now," he thought, "he will not get away from me. I will catch him on the spot."

Before Iván had walked two lengths of the fence it grew quite bright, and no longer in the former place, nor was it a small fire, but the flame licked up in the straw of the penthouse and was going toward the roof, and there stood Gavrílo so that the whole of him could be seen.

As a hawk swoops down on a lark, so Iván rushed up against Gavrílo the Lame.

"I will twist him up," he thought, "and he will not get away from me."

But Gavrílo the Lame evidently heard his steps and ran along the shed with as much speed as a hare.

"You will not get away," shouted Iván, swooping down on him.

He wanted to grab him by the collar, but Gavrílo got away from him, and Iván caught him by the skirt of his coat. The skirt tore off, and Iván fell down.

Iván jumped up.

"Help! Hold him!" and again he ran.

As he was getting up, Gavrílo was already near his yard, but Iván caught up with him. He was just going to take hold of him, when something stunned him, as though a stone had come down on his head. Gavrílo had picked up an oak post near his house and hit Iván with all his might on the head, when he ran up to him.

Iván staggered, sparks flew from his eyes, then all grew dark, and he fell down. When he came to his senses, Gavrílo was gone. It was as light as day, and from his yard came a sound as though an engine were working, and it roared and crackled there. Iván turned around and saw that his back shed was all on fire and the side shed was beginning to burn; the fire, and the smoke, and the burning straw were being carried toward the house.

"What is this? Friend!" cried Iván. He raised his hands and brought them down on his calves. "If I could only pull it out from the penthouse, and put it out! What is this? Friends!" he repeated. He wanted to shout, but he nearly strangled,—he had no voice. He wanted to run, but his feet would not move,—they tripped each other up. He tried to walk slowly, but he staggered, and he nearly strangled. He stood still again and drew breath, and started to walk. Before he came to the shed and reached the fire, the side shed was all on fire, and he could not get into the yard. People came running up, but nothing could be done. The neighbours dragged their own things out of their houses, and drove the cattle out. After Iván's house, Gavrílo's caught fire; a wind rose and carried the fire across the street. Half the village burned down.

All they saved from Iván's house was the old man, who

was pulled out, and everybody jumped out in just what they had on. Everything else was burned, except the horses in the pasture: the cattle were burned, the chickens on their roosts, the carts, the ploughs, the harrows, the women's chests, the grain in the granary,—everything was burned.

Gavrílo's cattle were saved, and they dragged a few things out of his house.

It burned for a long time, all night long. Iván stood near his yard, and kept looking at it, and saying:

"What is this? Friends! If I could just pull it out and put it out!"

But when the ceiling in the hut fell down, he jumped into the hottest place, took hold of a brand, and wanted to pull it out. The women saw him and began to call him back, but he pulled out one log and started for another: he staggered and fell on the fire. Then his son rushed after him and dragged him out. Iván had his hair and beard singed and his garments burnt and his hands blistered, but he did not feel anything.

"His sorrow has bereft him of his senses," people said.

The fire died down, but Iván was still standing there, and saying:

"Friends, what is this? If I could only pull it out."

In the morning the elder sent his son to Iván.

"Uncle Iván, your father is dying: he has sent for you, to bid you good-bye."

Iván had forgotten about his father, and did not understand what they were saying to him.

"What father?" he said. "Send for whom?"

"He has sent for you, to bid you good-bye. He is dying in our house. Come, Uncle Iván!" said the elder's son, pulling him by his arm.

Iván followed the elder's son.

When the old man was carried out, burning straw fell on him and scorched him. He was taken to the elder's house in a distant part of the village. This part did not burn.

When Iván came to his father, only the elder's wife was

there, and the children on the oven. The rest were all at the fire. The old man was lying on a bench, with a taper in his hand, and looking toward the door. When his son entered, he stirred a little. The old woman went up to him and said that his son had come. He told her to have him come closer to him. Iván went up, and then the old man said:

"What have I told you, Iván? Who has burned the village?"

"He, father," said Iván, "he,—I caught him at it. He put the fire to the roof while I was standing near. If I could only have caught the burning bunch of straw and put it out, there would not have been anything."

"Iván," said the old man, "my death has come, and you, too, will die. Whose sin is it?"

Iván stared at his father and kept silence; he could not say a word.

"Speak before God: whose sin is it? What have I told you?"

It was only then that Iván came to his senses, and understood everything. And he snuffled, and said:

"Mine, father." And he knelt before his father, and wept, and said: "Forgive me, father! I am guilty toward you and toward God."

The old man moved his hands, took the taper in his left hand, and was moving his right hand toward his brow, to make the sign of the cross, but he did not get it so far, and he stopped.

"Glory be to thee, O Lord! Glory be to thee, O Lord!" he said, and his eyes were again turned toward his son.

"Iván! Oh, Iván!"

"What is it, father?"

"What is to be done now?"

Iván was weeping.

"I do not know, father," he said. "How am I to live now, father?"

The old man closed his eyes and lisped something, as though

gathering all his strength, and he once more opened his eyes and said:

"You will get along. With God's aid will you get along." The old man was silent awhile, and he smiled and said:

"Remember, Iván, you must not tell who started the fire. Cover up another man's sin! God will forgive two sins."

And the old man took the taper into both hands, folded them over his heart, heaved a sigh, stretched himself, and died.

Iván did not tell on Gavrílo, and nobody found out how the fire had been started.

And Iván's heart was softened toward Gavrílo, and Gavrílo marvelled at Iván, because he did not tell anybody. At first Gavrílo was afraid of him, but later he got used to him. The peasants stopped quarrelling, and so did their families. While they rebuilt their homes, the two families lived in one house, and when the village was built again, and the farmhouses were built farther apart, Iván and Gavrílo again were neighbours, living in the same block.

And Iván and Gavrílo lived neighbourly together, just as their fathers had lived. Iván Shcherbakóv remembered his father's injunction and God's command to put out the fire in the beginning. And if a person did him some harm, he did not try to have his revenge on the man, but to mend matters; and if a person called him a bad name, he did not try to answer with worse words still, but to teach him not to speak badly. And thus he taught also the women folk and the children. And Iván Shchlerbakóv improved and began to live better than ever.

CHRISTIANITY AND PATRIOTISM

(1894)

THE Franco-Russian celebrations which took place in France, in the month of October of last year, provoked in me, as no doubt in many other people, at first a feeling of amusement, then of perplexity, and at last of indignation, which I intended to express in a short article in a periodical; but, the more I dwelt on the chief causes of this strange phenomenon, the more did I arrive at the considerations which I now offer to my readers.

I.

RUSSIANS and Frenchmen have lived for many centuries, knowing one another, entering with one another at times into friendly, more often, I am sorry to say, into very hostile relations, which have been provoked by their governments; suddenly, because two years ago a French squadron arrived at Kronstadt, and the officers of the squadron, upon landing, ate and drank a lot of wine in various places, hearing and uttering upon these occasions many lying and stupid words, and because, in the year 1893, a similar Russian squadron arrived at Toulon, and the officers of the Russian squadron ate and drank a lot in Paris, hearing and uttering upon that occasion more lying and stupid words than before, it happened that not only the men who ate, drank, and talked, but even those who were present, and even those who were not present, but only heard and read of it in newspapers, all these millions of Russians and Frenchmen suddenly imagined that they somehow were particularly in love with one another, that is, that all the French loved all the Russians, and all the Russians loved all the French.

These sentiments were last October expressed in France in a most unusual manner.

Here is the way the reception of the Russian sailors is described in the *Rural Messenger,* a newspaper which collects its information from all the others:

"At the meeting of the Russian and French vessels, both, besides the salvos of guns, greeted one another with hearty, ecstatic shouts, 'Hurrah,' 'Long live Russia,' 'Long live France!'

"These were joined by bands of music (which came on many private steamers), playing the Russian hymn, 'God save the Tsar,' and the French Marseillaise; the public on the private vessels waved their hats, flags, handkerchiefs, and bouquets; on many barques there were peasants with their wives and children, and they all had bouquets in their hands, and even the children waved the bouquets and shouted at the top of their voices, *'Vive la Russie!'* Our sailors, upon seeing such national transport, were unable to restrain their tears. . . .

"In the harbour all the ships-of-war which were then at Toulon were drawn out in two lines, and our squadron passed between them; in front was the ironclad of the admiralty, and this was followed by the rest. There ensued a most solemn minute.

"On the Russian ironclad, fifteen salvos were fired in honour of the French squadron, and a French ironclad replied with double the number, with thirty salvos. From the French vessels thundered the sounds of the Russian hymn. The French sailors climbed up on the sail-yards and masts; loud exclamations of greeting proceeded uninterruptedly from the two squadrons and from the private vessels; the caps of the sailors, the hats and handkerchiefs of the public,—all were thrown up triumphantly in honour of the dear guests. On all sides, on the water and on the shore, there boomed one common call, 'Long live Russia! Long live France!'

"In conformity with naval law, Admiral Avelán and the officers of his staff landed, in order to greet the local authorities. On the quay the Russian sailors were met by the chief marine staff of France and the superior officers of the port of Toulon. There ensued a universal friendly hand-shaking, accompanied by the boom of cannon and the ringing of bells. A band of marine music played the hymn 'God save the Tsar,' drowned by the thunderous shouts of the public, 'Long live the Tsar! Long live Russia!' These exclamations blended into one mighty sound, which drowned the music and the salvos from the guns.

"Eye-witnesses declare that at this moment the enthusiasm of the innumerable mass of people reached its highest limits, and that it is impossible to express in words with what sensations the hearts of all those present were filled. Admiral Avelán, with bared head, and accompanied by Russian and French officers, directed his steps to the building of the Marine Office, where the French minister of marine was waiting for him.

"In receiving the admiral, the minister said: 'Kronstadt and Toulon are two places which bear witness to the sympathy between the Russian and the French nations; you will everywhere be met as dear friends. The government and all of France welcome you upon your arrival and that of your companions, who represent a great and noble nation.'

"The admiral replied that he was not able to express all his gratitude. 'The Russian squadron and all of Russia,' he said, will remember the reception you have given us.'

"After a short conversation, the admiral, saying good-bye to the minister, a second time thanked him for the reception, and added, 'I do not want to part from you before pronouncing those words which are imprinted in all Russian hearts: "Long live France." ' " (*Rural Messenger*, 1893, No. 41.)

Such was the meeting at Toulon. In Paris the meeting and the celebrations were more remarkable still.

Here is the way the meeting in Paris was described in the newspapers: "All eyes were directed to the Boulevard des

Italiens, whence the Russian sailors were to appear. Finally
the boom of a whole hurricane of exclamations and applauses
is heard in the distance. The boom grows stronger and more
audible. The hurricane is apparently approaching. A mighty
motion takes place on the square. Policemen rush forward to
clear a path toward the Cercle Militaire, but this is by no
means an easy task. There is an incredible crush and pressure
in the crowd. . . . Finally the head of the• procession appears in the square. At the same moment a deafening shout,
'*Vive la Russie! Vive les Russes!*' rises over it. All bare their
heads, the public, packed close in the windows, on the bal-
conies, perched even on the roofs, wave handkerchiefs, flags,
and hats, applaud madly, and from the windows of the upper
stories throw clouds of small many-coloured cockades. A
whole sea of handkerchiefs, hats, and flags surges above the
heads of the crowd in the square: '*Vive la Russie! Vive les
Russes!*' shouts this mass of one hundred thousand people,
trying to get a look at the dear guests, extending their hands
to them, and in every way expressing their sympathies." (*New
Time*.)

Another correspondent writes that the transport of the
crowd bordered on delirium. A Russian publicist, who was
in Paris at that time, describes this entrance of the sailors
in the following manner: "They tell the truth,—it was an
incident of world-wide import, wondrous, touching, soul-
stirring, making the heart quiver with that love which
discerns the brothers in men, and which detests bloodshed
and concomitant acts of violence, the tearing away of the
children from their beloved mother. I have been in some kind
of an intoxication for several hours. I felt so strange, and
even so weak, as I stood at the station of the Lyons Rail-
way, among the representatives of the French administration
in their gold-embroidered uniforms, among the members of
the municipality in full dress, and heard the shouts, '*Vive la
Russie! Vive le Czar!*' and our national hymn, which was
played several times in succession. Where am I? What has
happened? What magic stream has united all this into

one feeling, into one mind? Does one not feel here the presence of the God of love and brotherhood, the presence of something higher, something ideal, which descends upon men only in lofty moments? The heart is so full of something beautiful and pure and exalted, that the pen is not able to express it all. Words pale before what I saw, what I felt. It is not transport,—the word is too banal,—it is something better than transport. It is more picturesque, profounder, more joyous, more varied. It is impossible to describe what happened at the Cercle Militaire, when Admiral Avelán appeared on the balcony of a second story. Words will not tell anything here. During the Te Deum, when the choristers sang in the church 'Save, O Lord, thy people,' there burst through the open door the solemn sounds of the Marseillaise, which was played in the street by an orchestra of wind-instruments. There was something astounding and inexpressible in the impression conveyed." (*New Time,* October, 1893.)

II.

AFTER arriving in France, the Russian sailors for two weeks went from one celebration to another, and in the middle or at the end of every celebration they ate, drank and talked; and the information as to what they ate and drank on Wednesday and where and what on Friday, and what was said upon that occasion, was wired home and conveyed to the whole of Russia. The moment some Russian captain drank the health of France, this at once became known to the whole world, and the moment the Russian admiral said, "I drink to fair France!" these words were immediately borne over the whole world. But more than that: the scrupulousness of the newspapers was such that they reported not only the toasts, but even many dinners, with the cakes and appetizers which were used at these dinners.

They reported also the speeches which were made by the celebrators, but the menus were more varied than the speeches. The speeches consisted invariably of the same words in all kinds of combinations and permutations. The meaning of these words was always one and the same: "We love one another tenderly, we are in transport, because we have so suddenly fallen in love with one another. Our aim is not war and not *revanche*, and not the return of provinces taken, but only *peace*, the benefaction of *peace*, the security of *peace*, the rest and *peace* of Europe. Long live the Emperor of Russia and the empress,—we love them and we love *peace*. Long live the president of the republic and his wife,—we love them, too, and we love *peace*. Long live France, Russia, their fleets, and their armies. We love the army, too, and *peace*, and the chief of the squadron." The speeches generally ended, as in couplets, with the words, "Toulon, Kronstadt," or "Kronstadt, Toulon." And the names of these places, where so much food was eaten and so many kinds of wine were consumed, were pronounced like words reminding one of the loftiest, most valorous of acts of the representatives of both nations, words after which there was nothing else to be said, because everything was comprehensible. "We love one another, and we love peace. Kronstadt, Toulon!" What else can be added to this? Especially with the accompaniment of solemn music, playing simultaneously two hymns, one—praising the Tsar and asking God for all kinds of benefactions for him, and the other—cursing all kings and promising their ruin.

The men who expressed their sentiments of love particularly well received decorations and rewards; other men for the same services, or simply out of a superabundance of feelings, were given the strangest and most unexpected presents,—thus the Emperor of Russia received from the French squadron some kind of a golden book, in which, I think, nothing was written, and if there was, it was something that nobody needed to know, and the chief of the Russian squadron received, among other presents, a still more remarkable object, an aluminum plough, covered with flowers, and many other just as unexpected presents.

Besides, all these strange acts were accompanied by still

stranger religious ceremonies and public prayers, which, it would seem, the French had long ago outlived. Since the days of the Concordat there had hardly been offered so many prayers as in that short time. All the French suddenly became unusually pious, and carefully hung up in the rooms of the Russian sailors those very images which they had just as carefully removed from their schools, as being harmful tools of superstition, and they kept praying all the time. Cardinals and bishops everywhere prescribed prayers, and themselves prayed, uttering the strangest prayers. Thus the Bishop of Toulon at the launching of the ironclad *Joriguiberi* prayed to the God of peace, making people feel, however, that if it came to a pinch, he could address also the God of war.

"What her fate will be," said the bishop, in reference to the ironclad, "God alone knows. No one knows whether she will belch forth death from her appalling bosom. But if, invoking now the God of peace, we should later have occasion to invoke the God of war, we are firmly convinced that the *Joriguiberi* will go forth side by side with the mighty boats whose crews have this day entered into such a close fraternal union with our own. Far from us be such a prospect, and may the present festivity leave nothing but a peaceful recollection, like the recollection of the *Grand Duke Constantine,* who was present here (in 1857) at the launching of the ship *Quirinal,* and may the friendship of France and of Russia make these two nations the guardians of peace."

In the meantime tens of thousands of telegrams flew from Russia to France, and from France to Russia. French women greeted Russian women. Russian women expressed their gratitude to the French women. A troupe of Russian actors greeted some French actors, and the French actors informed them that they harboured deeply in their hearts the greeting of the Russian actors. Some Russian candidates for judicial positions, who served in a Circuit Court of some town or other, expressed their enthusiasm for the French nations. General So and So thanked Madame So and So, and Madame So

and So assured General So and and So of her sentiments for the
Russian nation; Russian children wrote verses of welcome to
French children, and the French children answered in verse
and in prose; the Russian minister of education assured the
French minister of education of the sentiments of sudden
love for the French, which were experienced by all the
children, scholars, and authors subject to his ministry; members of a society for the protection of animals expressed their
ardent attachment for the French, and so did the Council
of the City of Kazán.

The canon of the eparchy of Arras informed his Worship,
the chief priest of the Russian court clergy, that he could
affirm that deep in the hearts of all the French cardinals
and archbishops there was imprinted a love for Russia and
his Majesty Alexander III. and his most august family, and
that the Russian and French clergy professed almost the
selfsame religion and equally honoured the Virgin; to which
his Worship, the chief priest, replied that the prayers of the
French clergy for the most august family reëchoed joyfully
in the hearts of the whole Russian Tsar-loving family, and
that, since the Russian people also worshipped the Holy
Virgin, it could count on France in life and in death. Almost
the same information was vouchsafed by different generals,
telegraph operators, and dealers in groceries. Everybody con-
gratulated somebody on something and thanked somebody
for something.

The excitement was so great that the most unusual acts
were committed, but no one observed their unusual character,
and all, on the contrary, approved of them, went into ecstasies
over them, and, as though fearing lest they should be too late,
hastened to commit similar acts, so as not to fall behind the
rest. If protests were expressed in words and in writing
and in printing against these mad acts, pointing out their irrationality, such protests were concealed or squelched.[1]

[1] Thus I know of the following protest of students, sent to Paris, which
was not accepted by a single newspaper:
" OPEN LETTER TO THE FRENCH STUDENTS
" Lately a group of Moscow students of law, with the university authori-

To say nothing of all the millions of work-days which were wasted on these festivities, of the wholesale drunkenness of all the participants, which was encouraged by all the powers, to say nothing of the insipidity of the speeches made, the maddest and most cruel things were done, and no one paid any attention to them.

Thus several dozens of men were crushed to death, and no one found it necessary to mention this fact. One correspondent wrote that a Frenchman told him at a ball that now there could hardly be found a woman in Paris who would not be false to her duties, in order to satisfy the wishes

ties at their head, took it upon themselves to speak in behalf of all the student body of Moscow University in respect to the Toulon festivities.

"We, the representatives of the association of student societies, protest in the most emphatic manner possible both against the arrogation of this group and substantially against the exchange of civilities between it and the French students. We, too, look with ardent love and profound respect upon France, and we do so, because we see in it a great nation, which formerly used to appear before the whole world as the herald and proclaimer of great ideals of liberty, equality, and fraternity; and which was also the first in the matter of bold endeavour for the materialization of these great ideals,— and the best part of the Russian youth has always been ready to welcome France as the leading champion for the best future of humanity; but we do not consider such festivities as those of Kronstadt and Toulon a suitable occasion for such civilities.

"On the contrary, these festivities signal a sad but, let us hope, temporary phenomenon,—the disloyalty of France to its former great historic rôle: the country, which once called the whole world to break the fetters of despotism and offered its fraternal aid to every nation that revolted for the sake of its freedom, now burns incense before the Russian government, which systematically trigs the normal, organic, and vital growth of the national life, and mercilessly crushes, without stopping at anything, all the strivings of Russian society toward the light, toward freedom, and toward independence. The Toulon manifestations are one of the acts of that drama which is presented by the antagonism—the creation of Napoleon III and Bismarck —between two great nations, France and Germany. This antagonism keeps all of Europe under arms, and makes the Russian absolutism, which has always been the stay of despotism and arbitrariness against freedom, of the exploiters against the exploited, the executor of the political destinies of the world. A sensation of anguish for our country, of pity for the blindness of a considerable part of French society, such are the sensations evoked in us by these festivities.

"We are fully convinced that the young generation of France will not be carried away by the national Chauvinism, and that, prepared to struggle for that better social structure toward which humanity is marching, it will know how to render to itself an account of the present events and to take the proper stand about them; we hope that our fervent protest will find a sympathetic echo in the hearts of the French youth.

"The union council of twenty-four united Moscow student societies."— *Author's Note.*

of some Russian sailor—and all this passed by unnoticed, as something that ought to be. There occurred cases of distinct madness. Thus one woman, dressing herself in a garment of colours of the Franco-Russian flags, waited for the sailors and, exclaiming, "*Vive la Russie!*" jumped from the bridge into the river and was drowned.

Women in general played in these festivities a prominent part and even guided the men. Besides throwing flowers and all kinds of ribbons, and offering presents and addresses, French women made for the Russian sailors and kissed them; some of them for some reason brought their children to them, to be kissed by them, and when the Russian sailors complied with their wish, all persons present went into ecstasies and wept.

This strange excitement was so infectious that, as one correspondent tells, an apparently absolutely sound Russian sailor, after two days of contemplation of what took place around him, in the middle of the day jumped from the ship into the sea and, swimming, shouted, "*Vive la France!*" When he was taken aboard and asked why he had done so, he replied that he had made a vow that in honour of France he would swim around the ship.

In answering a toast at a dinner given in the Palace of the Elysées, the Russian ambassador said: "Before drinking a toast to which will respond from the depth of their hearts, not only those who are within these walls, but even those—and, that, too, with equal force—whose hearts near by and far away, at all the points of great, fair France, as also in all of Russia, at the present moment are beating in unison with ours,—permit me to offer to you the expression of our profoundest gratitude for the words of welcome which were addressed by you to our admiral, whom our Tsar has charged with the mission of paying back your visit at Kronstadt. Considering the high importance which you enjoy, your words characterize the true significance of the magnificent *peaceful* festivities, which are celebrated with such wonderful unanimity, loyalty, and sincerity."

The same unjustifiable mention of peace is found in the speech of the French president: "The ties of love, which unite Russia and France," he said, "and which two years ago were strengthened by touching manifestations, of which our fleet was the object at Kronstadt, become tighter and tighter with every day, and the honourable exchange of our amicable sentiments must inspire all those who take to heart the benefactions of peace, confidence, and security," and so forth.

Both speeches quite unexpectedly and without any cause refer to the benefactions of peace and to peaceful celebrations.

There is not one speech, not one article, in which mention is not made of this, that the aim of all these past orgies is the peace of Europe. At a dinner, which is given by the representatives of the Russian press, everybody speaks of peace. Mr. Zola, who lately wrote about the necessity and even usefulness of war, and Mr. Vogüé, who more than once expressed the same idea, do not say one word about war, but speak only of peace. The meetings of the Chambers are opened with speeches respecting the past celebrations, and the orators affirm that these festivities are the declaration of the peace of Europe.

It is as though a man, coming into some peaceful society, should go out of his way on every occasion to assure the persons present that he has not the slightest intention of knocking out anybody's teeth, smashing eyes, or breaking arms, but means only to pass a peaceable evening. "But nobody has any doubts about that," one feels like saying to him. "But if you have such base intentions, at least do not dare speak of them to us."

In many articles, which were written about these celebrations, there is even a direct and naïve expression of pleasure, because during the festivities no one gave utterance to what by tacit consent it had been decided to conceal from everybody, and what only one incautious man, who was immediately removed by the police, dared to shout, giving expression to the secret thought of all, namely, "*A bas l'Allemagne!*" Thus children are frequently so happy at having concealed their naughtiness, that their very joy gives them away.

Why should we so rejoice at the fact that no mention was made of war, if we indeed are not thinking of it?

III.

No one is thinking of war, but yet milliards are wasted on military preparations, and, millions of men are under arms in Russia and in France.

"But all this is being done for the security of peace. *Si vis pacem, para bellum. L'empire c'est la paix, la république, c'est la paix.*"

But if it is so, why are the military advantages of our alliance with France in case of a war with Germany explained, not only in all the periodicals and newspapers published for the so-called cultured people, but also in the *Rural Messenger*, a newspaper published by the Russian government for the masses, by means of which these unfortunate masses, deceived by the government, are impressed with this, that "to be friendly with France is also useful and profitable, because, if, beyond all expectation, the above-mentioned powers (Germany, Austria, Italy) should decide to violate the peace with Russia, Russia, though able with God's aid to protect itself and handle a very powerful alliance of adversaries, would not find this to be an easy task, and for a successful struggle great sacrifices and losses would be needed," and so forth (*Rural Messenger*, No. 43, 1893).

And why do they in all the French colleges teach history from a text-book composed by Mr. Lavisse, twenty-first edition, 1889, in which the following passage is found:

"*Depuis que l'insurrection de la Commune a été vaincue, la France n'a plus été troublée. Au lendemain de la guerre, elle s'est remise au travail. Elle a payé aux Allemands sans difficulté l'énorme contribution de guerre de cinq milliards. Mais la France a perdu sa renommée militaire pendant la guerre de 1870. Elle a perdu une partie de son territoire. Plus de quinze cents mille hommes, qui habitaient nos departe-*

ments du Haut Rhin, du Bas Rhin et de la Moselle, et qui étaient de bons Français, ont été obligés de devenir Allemands. Ils ne sont pas resignés à leur sort. Ils détestent l'Allemagne; ils espèrent toujours redevenir Français. Mais l'Allemagne tient à sa conquête, et c'est un grand pays, dont tous les habitants aiment sincèrement leur patrie et dont les soldats sont braves et disciplinés. Pour reprendre à l'Allemagne ce qu'elle nous a pris, il faut que nous soyons de bons citoyens et de bons soldats. C'est pour que vous deveniez de bons soldats, que vos maîtres vous apprennent l'histoire de la France. L'histoire de la France montre que dans notre pays les fils ont toujours vengé les désastres de leurs pères. Les Français du temps de Charles VII. ont vengé leurs pères vaincus à Crécy, à Poitiers, à Azincourt. C'est à vous, enfants élèves aujourd'hui dans nos écoles, qu'il appartient de venger vos pères, vaincus à Sédan et à Metz. C'est votre devoir, le grand devoir de votre vie. Vous devez y penser toujours," etc.

At the foot of the page there is a whole series of questions, to correspond to the articles. The questions are as follows: "What did France lose when she lost part of her territory? How many Frenchmen became German with the loss of this territory? Do the French love Germany? What must we do, in order to regain what was taken away from us by Germany?" In addition to these are also *"Réflexions sur le Livre VII.,"* in which it says that "the children of France must remember our defeats of 1870," that "they must feel on their hearts the burden of this memory," but that "this memory must not discourage them: it should, on the contrary, incite them to bravery."

Thus, if in official speeches peace is mentioned with great persistency, the masses, the younger generations, yes, all the Russians and Frenchmen in general, are imperturbably impressed with the necessity, legality, profitableness, and even virtue of war.

"We are not thinking of war,—we are concerned only about peace."

One feels like asking *"Qui, diable, trompe-t-on ici?"* if it

were necessary to ask this, and if it were not quite clear
who the unfortunate cheated are.

The cheated are the same eternally deceived, stupid, labouring masses, the same who with their callous hands have
built all these ships, fortresses, and arsenals, and barracks,
and guns, and steamboats, and quays, and moles, and all these
palaces, balls, and platforms, and triumphal arches; and have
set and printed all these newspapers and books; and have
secured and brought all these pheasants, and ortolans, and
oysters, and wines, which are consumed by all those men,
whom they, again, have nurtured and brought up and sus-
tained,—men who, deceiving the masses, prepare the most
terrible calamities for them; the same good-natured, stupid
masses, who, displaying their sound, white teeth, have grinned
in childish fashion, naïvely enjoying the sight of all the
dressed-up admirals and presidents, of the flags fluttering
above them, the fireworks, the thundering music, and who
will hardly have time to look around, when there shall be
no longer admirals, nor presidents, nor flags, nor music, but
there will be only a wet, waste field, hunger, cold, gloom, in
front the slaying enemy, behind the goading authorities, blood,
wounds, sufferings, rotting corpses, and a senseless, useless
death.

And the men like those who now are celebrating at the
festivities in Toulon and Paris, will be sitting, after a good
dinner, with unfinished glasses of good wine, with a cigar
between their teeth, in a dark cloth tent, and will with
pins mark down the places on the map where so much food for
cannon, composed of the masses, should be left, in order to
seize such and such a fortress, and in order to obtain such
or such a ribbon or promotion.

IV.

"But there is nothing of the kind, and there are no warlike
intentions," we are told. "All there is, is that two nations
feeling a mutual sympathy are expressing this sentiment to

one another. What harm is there in this, that the representatives of a friendly nation were received with especial solemn-
ity and honour by the representatives of the other nation?
What harm is there in it, even if it be admitted that the alliance may have the significance of a protection against a dangerous neighbour, threatening the peace of Europe?"

The harm is this, that all this is a most palpable and
bold lie, an unjustifiable, bad lie. The sudden outburst of an
exclusive love of the Russians for the French, and of the
French for the Russians, is a lie; and our hatred for the
Germans, our distrust of them, which is understood by it,
is also a lie. And the statement that the aim of all these
indecent and mad orgies is the guarantee of European peace,
is a still greater lie.

We all know that we have experienced no particular love
for the French, neither before, nor even now, even as we have
not experienced any hostile feeling toward the Germans.

We are told that Germany has some intentions against
Russia, that the Triple Alliance threatens the peace of Europe
and us, and that our alliance with France balances the forces,
and so guarantees the peace. But this assertion is so obviously
absurd, that it makes one feel ashamed to give it a serious
denial. For this to be so, that is, for the alliance to guarantee peace, it is necessary that the forces be mathematically
even. If now the excess is on the side of the Franco-Russian
alliance, the danger is still the same. It is even greater, because, if there was a danger that William, who stood at the
head of the European alliance, would violate the peace, there
is a much greater danger that France, which cannot get used
to the loss of her provinces, will do so. The Triple Alliance
was called a league of peace, but for us it was a league of war.
Even so now the Franco-Russian alliance cannot present
itself as anything else than what it is,—a league of war.

And then, if peace depends on the balance of the powers,
how are the units to be determined, between whom the balance is to be established? Now the English say that the
alliance between Russia and France menaces them, and

that they must, therefore, form another alliance. And into how many units of alliances must Europe be divided, in order that there be a balance? If so, then every man stronger than another in society is already a danger, and the others must form into alliances, to withstand him.

They ask, "What harm is there in this, that France and Russia have expressed their mutual sympathies for the guarantee of peace?" What is bad is, that it is a lie, and a lie is never spoken with impunity, and does not pass unpunished.

The devil is a slayer of men and the father of lies. And the lies always lead to the slaying of men,—in this case more obviously than ever.

In just the same manner as now, the Turkish war was preceded by a sudden outburst of love of our Russians for their brothers, the Slavs, whom no one had known for hundreds of years, while the Germans, the French, the English have always been incomparably nearer and more closely related to us than Montenegrins, Servians, or Bulgarians. And there began transports, receptions, and festivities, which were fanned by such men as Aksákov and Katkóv, who are mentioned now in Paris as models of patriotism. Then, as now, they spoke of nothing but the mutual sudden outburst of love between the Russians and the Slavs. In the beginning they ate and drank in Moscow, even as now in Paris, and talked nonsense to one another, becoming affected by their own exalted sentiments, spoke of union and peace, and did not say anything about the chief thing, the intentions against Turkey. The newspapers fanned the excitement, and the government by degrees entered into the game. Servia revolted. There began an exchange of diplomatic notes and the publication of semiofficial articles; the newspapers lied more and more, invented and waxed wroth, and the end of it all was that Alexander II., who really did not want any war, could not help but agree to it, and we all know what happened: the destruction of hundreds of thousands of innocent people and the bestialization and dulling of millions.

What was done in Toulon and in Paris, and now continues

to be done in the newspapers, obviously leads to the same, or to a still more terrible calamity. Just so all kinds of generals and ministers will at first, to the sounds of "God save the Tsar" and the Marseillaise drink the health of France, of Russia, of the various regiments of the army and the navy; the newspapers will print their lies; the idle crowd of the rich, who do not know what to do with their powers and with their time, will babble patriotic speeches, fanning hatred against Germany, and no matter how peaceful Alexander III. may be, the conditions will be such that he will be unable to decline a war which will be demanded by all those who surround him, by all the newspapers, and, as always seems, by the public opinion of the whole nation. And before we shall have had time to look around, there will appear in the columns of the newspapers the usual, ominous, stupid proclamation:

"By God's grace, we, the most autocratic great Emperor of all Russia, the King of Poland, the Grand Duke of Finland, etc., etc., inform all our faithful subjects that for the good of these dear subjects, entrusted to us by God, we have considered it our duty before God to send them out to slaughter. God be with them," and so forth.

The bells will be rung, and long-haired men will throw gold-embroidered bags over themselves and will begin to pray for the slaughter. And there will begin again the old, well-known, terrible deed. The newspaper writers, who under the guise of patriotism stir people up to hatred and murder, will be about, in the hope of double earnings. Manufacturers, merchants, purveyors of military supplies, will bestir themselves joyfully, expecting double profits. All kinds of officials will bestir themselves, foreseeing a chance to steal more than they usually do. The military authorities will bestir themselves, for they will receive double salaries and rations, and will hope to get for the killing of people all kinds of trifles, which they value very much,—ribbons, crosses, galloons, stars. Idle gentlemen and ladies will bestir themselves, inscribing themselves in advance in the Red Cross, preparing themselves to dress the wounds of those whom their own husbands and brothers will kill, and imagining that they are thus doing a most Christian work.

And, drowning in their hearts their despair by means of songs, debauches, and vódka, hundreds of thousands of simple, good people, torn away from peaceful labour, from their wives, mothers, children, will march, with weapons of murder in their hands, whither they will be driven. They will go to freeze, to starve, to be sick, to die from diseases, and finally they will arrive at the place where they will be killed by the thousand, and they will kill by the thousand, themselves not knowing why, men whom they have never seen and who have done them and can do them no harm.

And when there shall be collected so many sick, wounded, and killed that nobody will have the time to pick them up, and when the air shall already be so infected by this rotting food for cannon that even the authorities will feel uncomfortable, then they will stop for awhile, will somehow manage to pick up the wounded, will haul off and somewhere throw into a pile the sick, and will bury the dead, covering them with lime, and again they will lead on the whole crowd of the deceived, and will continue to lead them on in this manner until those who have started the whole thing will get tired of it, or until those who needed it will get what they needed.

And again will men become infuriated, brutalized, and bestialized, and love will be diminished in the world, and the incipient Christianization of humanity will be delayed for decades and for centuries. And again will the people, who gain thereby, begin to say with assurance that, if there is a war, this means that it is necessary, and again they will begin to prepare for it the future generations, by corrupting them from childhood.

V.

ABOUT four years ago,—the first swallow of the Toulon spring,—a certain French agitator in favour of a war with Germany came to Russia for the purpose of preparing the

Franco-Russian alliance, and he visited us in the country. He
arrived at our house when we were working in the mowing.
At breakfast, as we returned home, we made the acquaintance
of the guest, and he immediately proceeded to tell us how he
had fought, had been in captivity, had run away from it, and
how he had made a patriotic vow, of which he was apparently
proud, that he would not stop agitating a war against
Germany until the integrity and glory of France should be
reëstablished.

In our circle all the convictions of our guest as to how
necessary an alliance between Russia and France was for the
reëstablishment of the former borders of France and its
might and glory, and for making us secure against the malevo-
lent intentions of Germany, were of no avail to him. In
reply to his arguments that France could not be at peace
so long as the provinces taken from it were not returned
to it, we said that similarly Prussia could not be at rest, so
long as it had not paid back for Jena, and that, if the French
"revanche" should now be successful, the Germans would have
to pay them back, and so on without end.

In reply to his arguments that the French were obliged
to save their brothers, who had been torn away from them,
we said that the condition of the inhabitants, of the majority
of the inhabitants, of the working people in Alsace-Lorraine,
was hardly any worse under German rule than it had been
under France, and that, because some Alsatians preferred to
belong to France rather than to Germany, and he, our guest,
found it desirable to reëstablish the glory of French arms,
it was not worth while, either to begin those terrible calamities
which result from war, or even to sacrifice one single human
life.

In reply to his arguments that it was all very well for
us to speak thus, since we had not experienced the same, and
that we should be speaking differently, if we had the Baltic
provinces and Poland taken away from us, we said that even
from the political standpoint the loss of Poland and of the
Baltic provinces could not be a calamity for us, but might

rather be considered an advantage, since it would diminish the necessity for a military force and the expenses of state; and from the Christian point of view we never could permit a war, since a war demanded the killing of men, whereas Christianity not only forbade every murder, but even demanded that we do good to all men, considering all, without distinction of nationalities, as our brothers. The Christian state, we said, which enters upon war, to be consistent, must not only haul down the crosses from the churches, turn all the churches into buildings for different purposes, give the clergy other offices, and, above all, prohibit the Gospel, but must also renounce all the demands of morality which result from the Christian law. *"C'est à prendre ou à laisser,"* we said. But until Christianity was abolished, it would be possible to entice men to war only by cunning and deceit, as indeed is being done nowadays. We see this cunning and deception, and so cannot submit to it. As there was no music, no champagne, nothing intoxicating about us, our guest only shrugged his shoulders and with customary French amiability remarked that he was very thankful for the fine reception accorded to him in our house, but that he was sorry that his ideas were not treated in the same way.

VI.

AFTER this conversation we went to the mowing, and there he, in the hope of finding more sympathy for his ideas among the masses, asked me to translate to the peasant Prokófi, an old, sickly man, with an enormous rupture, who none the less stuck to his work, and was my companion in the mowing, his plan of attacking the Germans, which was to squeeze the Germans, who were between the French and the Russians, from both sides. The Frenchman gave an ocular demonstration of this to Prokófi, by touching from two sides Prokófi's sweaty hempen shirt with his white fingers. I recall Prokófi's good-naturedly scornful surprise, when I explained to him the Frenchman's words and gestures. The proposition to squeeze the Germans from both sides was apparently taken by Prokófi as a joke, for he would not admit the idea that a grown man and a scholar should calmly and when he was sober talk of the desirability of war.

"Well, if we squeeze the German from both sides," he replied jestingly to what he thought was a joke, "he will have no place to go to. We must give him room."

I translated this to my guest.

"*Dites lui que nous aimons les Russes,*" he said.

These words obviously startled Prokófi even more than the proposition to squeeze the German and provoked a certain sentiment of suspicion.

"Who is he?" Prokófi asked me, with mistrust, indicating my guest with his head.

I told him that he was a Frenchman, a rich man.

"What is his business?" Prokófi asked me.

When I explained to him that he had come to invite the Russians to form an alliance with France in case of a war with Germany, Prokófi apparently became quite dissatisfied, and, turning to the women, who were sitting near a haycock, he shouted at them in a strong voice, which involuntarily betrayed the feelings which this conversation had provoked in him, that they should go and rake up the unraked hay.

"Come now, you crows! Have you fallen asleep? Come! Much time we have to squeeze the German! We have not finished the mowing yet, and it looks likely that we shall be mowing on Wednesday," he said. And then, as though fearing to offend the stranger by such a remark, he added, displaying his half-worn-off teeth in a good-natured smile, "You had better come and work with us, and send the German, too. When we get through working, we shall have a good time. We'll take the German along. They are just such folk as we are." And having said this, Prokófi took his muscular arm out of the crotch of the fork, on which he had been leaning, threw the fork over his shoulders, and went away to the women.

"*Oh, le brave homme!*" the polite Frenchman exclaimed,

smiling. And with this he then concluded his diplomatic mission to the Russian people.

The sight of these so radically different men,—the one beaming with freshness, alacrity, elegance, the well-fed Frenchman, in a silk hat and long overcoat of the latest fashion, energetically illustrating with his white hands, unused to labour, how to squeeze the Germans, and the sight of the dishevelled Prokófi, with hay-seed in his hair, dried up from work, sunburnt, always tired and always working, in spite of his immense rupture, with fingers swollen from work, with his loosely hanging homespun trousers, battered bast shoes, jogging along with an immense forkful of hay over his shoulder in that indolent pace of a labouring man, which economizes motion,—the sight of these two so radically different men elucidated to me then many things, and has occurred to me now, after the Toulon-Paris celebrations. One of them personified to me those men, nurtured by the labours of the masses, who later use these masses as food for cannon; and Prokófi personified to me that food for cannon, which nurtures and makes secure the men who dispose of it.

TWO WARS

(1898)

Two wars are at the present•time being waged in the Christian world. One, it is true, has been ended, while the other is still going on; but they were waged at one and the same time, and the contrast between the two is striking. The first, now ended, was an old, vainglorious, stupid, cruel, untimely, obsolete, pagan war, the Spanish-American War, which by the murder of one set of men decided how and by whom another set of men was to be ruled. The second war, which is still going on, and which will be ended only when all wars shall end, is a new, self-sacrificing, sacred war, which is based on nothing but love and reason, the war against war, which (as Victor Hugo expressed it at one of the congresses) the best, most advanced part of the Christian humanity declared long ago against the other, the coarse and savage part of the same humanity, and which a handful of Christian men, the Dukhobors of the Caucasus, have of late waged with particular force and success against the powerful Russian government.

The other day I received a letter from Colorado, from a Mr. Jesse Glodwin, who asks me to send him "a few words or thoughts, expressive of my sentiments, in regard to the noble work of the American nation and the heroism of her soldiers and sailors." This gentleman is, with the vast majority of the American nation, fully convinced that the action of the Americans, which is, that they beat a few thousands of almost unarmed men (in comparison with the armament of the Americans the Spaniards were almost unarmed), is unquestionably a "noble work," and that those people who, having killed a large number of their neighbours, for the most part survived and were well and fixed themselves comfortably in life, were heroes.

The Spanish-American War, to say nothing of the horrible things which the Spaniards had done in Cuba, and which served as the pretext for the war, resembles this:

A decrepit and doting old man, who was brought up in the traditions of false honour, to settle a misunderstanding that arose between him and a young man, challenges this young man, who is in the full possession of his strength, to fisticuffs; and the young man, who, to judge from his past and from what he has said more than once, ought to stand incomparably higher than such a settlement of the question, accepts the challenge with knuckles in his clenched fist, jumps upon the decrepit and doting old man, knocks out his teeth, breaks his ribs, and then ecstatically tells his exploits to a vast public of just such young men as he is, and this public rejoices and praises the hero who has maimed the old man.

Such is the one war which occupied the minds of all in the Christian world. Nobody speaks of the other war; hardly any one knows anything about it. The other war is like this:

All the states deceive the people, saying: "All of you who are ruled by me are in danger of being conquered by other nations; I look after your well-being and security, and so demand that you shall annually give me millions of roubles, the fruits of your labours, which I am going to use for rifles, cannon, powder, ships for your defense; I demand, besides, that you shall enter the organizations instituted by me, where they will make of you senseless particles of an immense machine,—the army,—which I manage. While connected with this army you will cease being men and having your own will, but will do everything I want you to do. What I want to do first of all is to rule, and the means I use for ruling is murder; and so I am going to teach you to commit murder."

In spite of the obvious insipidity of the assertion that men are in danger from the attack of the governments of other

states, which assert that they, in spite of their desire for peace,
are in the same danger; in spite of the degradation of that
slavery to which men are subjected when they enter the
army; in spite of the cruelty of the business to which they
are called, men submit to the deception, give up their money
for their own enslavement, and themselves enslave one another.

And here there appear people who say:

"What you say of the threatening danger and of your con-
cern about protecting us against it is a deception. All the
states affirm that they want peace, and at the same time arm
themselves against one another. Besides, according to the
law which you profess, all men are brothers, and it makes
no difference whether we belong to this state or to another,
and so the attack of other states upon us, with which you
frighten us, has no terror and no meaning for us. But the
main thing is this, that, according to the law which was
given to us by God, and which you, too, profess, who demand of us a participation in murder, we are clearly forbidden
to commit murder or even any acts of violence, and so we
cannot and will not take part in your preparations for murder, will not give you any money for the purpose, and will
not join the gangs established by you, where you corrupt
the reason and the conscience of men, by changing them into
instruments of violence, who are submissive to every evil
man taking this instrument into his hands."

In this consists the second war, which has for a long
time been waged with the representatives of rude force, and
which of late has burned up with particular virulence between the Dukhobors and the Russian government. The Russian government has brought out against the Dukhobors all
those instruments with which it can fight. These instruments are: the police measures of arrests, the prohibition of
leaving the place of abode, the prohibition of intercommunication, the seizure of letters, espionage, the prohibition of
printing in the newspapers any information on matters per-
taining to the Dukhobors, calumny of them, printed in the

periodicals, bribery, flogging, prisons, deportation, the ruin of families. But the Dukhobors, on their side, have put forth nothing but their own religious instrument, meek, reason-ableness and long-suffering firmness, and say: "We must not obey men more than God, and no matter what they may do, we cannot and will not obey them."

They praise the Spanish and American heroes of that sav-age war, who, wishing to distinguish themselves in the eyes of men and to receive rewards and glory, have killed a very large number of men, or themselves have died in the process of slaying their neighbours. But no one speaks or knows of these heroes of the war against war, who are not seen and heard by any one, who have died under rods or in stinking cells, or in oppressive exile, and still to their very last breath remain true to the good and to truth.

I know of dozens of these martyrs who have died, and hun-dreds who, scattered over the whole world, continue this martyrs' profession of the truth.

I know Drózhzhin, a peasant teacher, who was tortured to death in the disciplinary battalion; I know another, Izyumchénko, Drózhzhin's companion, who was kept awhile in the disciplinary battalion and then was sent away to the end of the world; I know Olkhóvik, a peasant, who refused to do military service, was for this sentenced to be sent to the disciplinary battalion, and on the boat, converted his guard, Seredá. Seredá, who understood what Olkhóvik said about the sin of military service, came to the authorities and said, as the ancient martyrs said: "I do not want to be with the tor-menters, join me to the martyrs," and they began to torture him, sent him to the disciplinary battalion, and then to Yakútsk Territory. I know dozens of Dukhobors, many of whom have died or grown blind, who none the less do not submit to the demands which are contrary to the law of God.

The other day I read a letter about a young Dukhobor who was sent by himself, without any companions, to a regiment stationed in Samarkand. Again the same demands on the part of the authorities, and the same simple, unswerving

answers: "I cannot do what is contrary to my faith in God."
—"We will torture you to death."—"That is your business.
You do your business, and I will do mine."

And this twenty-year-old boy, cast by himself into a
foreign country, amidst hostile people, strong, rich, cultured
people, who direct all their forces to conquering him, does not
succumb and does his great work.

They say: "These are useless sacrifices. These men will
perish, but the structure of life will remain the same." Even
thus, I think, people spoke of the uselessness of Christ's sacrifice and of the sacrifice of all the martyrs for the sake of
truth. The people of our time, especially the scholars, have
become so gross that they do not understand, and in their
grossness cannot even understand, the significance and the
influence of spiritual force. A charge of ten thousand pounds
of dynamite sent into a crowd of living men,—that they
understand, and in that they see strength; but an idea, truth,
which has been realized, has been introduced into life to
the point of martyrdom, has become accessible to millions,—
that is according to their conception not force, because it
does not boom, and you do not see broken bones and puddles
of blood. Scholars (it is true, bad scholars) use all the
power of their erudition to prove that humanity lives like
a herd, which is guided only by economic conditions, and that
reason is given to it only for amusement; but the governments
know what it is that moves the world, and so unerringly,
from a sense of self-preservation, look most zealously upon
the manifestation of spiritual forces, on which depends their
existence or their ruin. For this reason all the efforts of the
Russian government have been directed upon making the Dukhobors harmless, upon isolating them and sending them abroad.

But, in spite of all their efforts, the struggle of the Dukhobors has opened the eyes of millions.

I know hundreds of old and young military men who,
thanks to the persecutions of the meek, industrious Dukhobors, have had misgivings as to the legality of their own
activity; I know people who for the first time reflected upon

life and the significance of Christianity, when they saw the life of these people or heard of the persecutions to which they have been subjected.

And the government, which rules over millions of people, knows this and feels that it has been struck at its very heart.

Such is the second war, which is being waged in our time, and such are its consequences. Its consequences are of importance, and not for the Russian government alone. Every government which is based on the army and on violence is struck in the same way by this weapon. Christ said, "I have conquered the world." He has really conquered the world, if people will only believe in the power of this weapon which is given to them.

This weapon is, for each man to follow his own reason and conscience.

This is so simple, so indubitable and obligatory for every single man. "You want to make me a participant in murder. You demand of me money for the preparation of the implements of murder, and you want me to become a participant in the organized gathering of murderers," says a rational man, who has not sold or dimmed his conscience. "But I confess the same law with you, in which not only murder, but even every hostility, has long ago been forbidden, and so I cannot obey you."

It is this means, which is so simple, that conquers the world. *Yásnaya Polyána, August 15, 1898.*

LETTER TO A CORPORAL

(1899)

You wonder how it is soldiers are taught that it is right to kill men in certain cases and in war, whereas in the Scripture, which is acknowledged to be sacred by those who teach this, there is nothing resembling such a permission, but there is the very opposite,—a prohibition to commit murder and even any insult against men, a prohibition to do to others what one does not wish to have done to oneself; you ask me whether this is not a deception, and if so, for whose advantage it is practiced.

Yes, it is a deception, which is practiced in favour of those who are accustomed to live by the sweat and blood of other people, and who for this purpose have been distorting Christ's teaching, which was given men for their good, but which now, in its distorted form, has become the chief source of all the calamities of men.

This happened in the following way:

The government and all those men of the upper classes who adhere to the government and live by the labours of others have to have means for controlling the labouring masses; the army is such a means. The defence against foreign enemies is only an excuse. The German government frightens its nation with the Russians and the French; the French frightens its nation with the Germans; the Russian frightens its nation with the Germans and the French, and so it is with all the nations; but neither the Germans, nor the Russians, nor the French wish to fight with their neighbours and with other nations; they prefer to live in peace with them and are afraid of war more than of anything in

45

the world. But, to have an excuse in their control of the labouring masses, the governments and the upper idle classes act like a gipsy, who whips his horse around the corner and then pretends that he is not able to hold it back. They stir up their people and another government, and then pretend that for the good or for the defence of their nation they cannot help but declare war, which again is profitable for the generals, officers, officials, merchants, and, in general, for the wealthy classes. In reality, war is only an inevitable consequence of the existence of the armies; but the armies are needed by the governments merely for the purpose of controlling their own labouring masses.

It is a criminal business, but the worst thing about it is this, that the governments, to have a rational foundation for their control of the masses, are obliged to pretend that they are professing the highest religious teaching known to men, that is, the Christian, and in this teaching educate their subjects. This teaching is in its essence opposed, not only to every murder, but even to every violence, and so, to be able to control the masses and be considered Christian, the governments had to distort Christianity and to conceal its true meaning from the masses and thus to deprive men of the good which Christ brought to them.

This distortion of Christianity took place long ago, in the time of the malefactor, Emperor Constantine, who for this was canonized a saint. All the subsequent governments, especially our own Russian government, have tried with all their strength to maintain this distortion and not to allow the masses to see the true meaning of Christianity, because, if they saw it, they would come to understand that the governments, with their taxes, soldiers, prisons, gallows, and cheating priests, are not only no pillars of Christianity, such as they pretend to be, but its greatest enemies.

In consequence of this distortion there result those deceptions which startled you so much, and all those terrible calamities from which the masses suffer.

The masses are crushed, robbed, impoverished, ignorant,—

they are dying out. Why? Because the land is in the hands of the rich; because the masses are enslaved in factories, in plants in their daily occupations; because they are fleeced for the taxes, and the price for their labour is lowered, and the price for what they need is raised. How can they be freed? Shall the land again be taken away from the rich? But if that is done, the soldiers will come, will kill off the rioters, and will lock them up in prisons. Shall the factories, the plants, be taken away? The same will happen. Stick out in a strike? But that will never happen,—the rich can stick out longer than the labourers, and the armies will always be on the side of the capitalists. The masses will never get away from that want in which they are held, so long as the armies shall be in the power of the ruling classes.

But who are the armies, which hold the masses in this slavery? Who are those soldiers who will shoot at the peasants who have taken possession of the land, and at the strikers, if they do not disperse, and at the smugglers, who import wares without paying the revenue,—who will put into prisons and keep there those who refuse to pay the taxes? These soldiers are the same peasants whose land has been taken away, the same strikers, who want to raise their wages, the same payers of the taxes, who want to be freed from these payments.

Why do these men shoot at their brothers? Because it has been impressed upon them that the oath which they are compelled to take upon entering military service is obligatory for them, and that they may not kill men in general, but may kill them by command of the authorities, that is, the same deception which startled so much is practiced upon them. But here arises the question,—how can people of sound mind, who frequently know the rudiments and are even educated, believe in such a palpable lie? No matter how little educated a man may be, he none the less cannot help knowing that Christ did not permit any murder, but taught meekness, humility, forgiveness of offenses, love of enemies; he cannot help but see that on the basis of the Christian teach-

ing he cannot make a promise in advance that he will kill all
those whom he is commanded to kill.

The question is, how can people of sound mind believe, as
all those who are now doing military service have believed,
in such an obvious deception? The answer to the question is
this, that people are not deceived by this one deception alone,
but have been prepared for it from childhood by a whole
series of deceptions, a whole system of deceptions, which is
called the Orthodox Church, and which is nothing but the
coarsest kind of idolatry. According to this faith men are
taught that God is triune, that besides this triune God there
is also a heavenly queen, and that in addition to this queen
there are also all kinds of saints, whose bodies have not de-
cayed, and that in addition to the saints there are also the
images of the Gods and of the queen of heaven, before which
tapers have to be placed and prayers made with the hands,
and that the most important and holy thing on earth is the
pap which the priest makes on Sundays back of the partition
out of wine and bread, that after the priest has whispered
something over this, the wine will not be wine and the bread
will not be bread, but the blood and body of one of the triune
Gods, and so forth. All that is so stupid and senseless that
it is absolutely impossible to understand what it all means,
and, indeed, those who teach this faith command us not to
understand, but to believe it; and the people, who have been
trained from childhood to believe this, believe any senseless
thing that they may be told. But after men are so stultified that they believe that God is hanging in the corner
or is sitting in the piece of pap which the priest is giving
them in a spoon, that it is useful for this life and for the life
to come to kiss a board or the relics and to place tapers before them, they are called upon to do military service, and
there they are deceived any way they are to be deceived, by
being compelled first of all to swear on the Gospel (which
prohibits swearing) that they will do what is prohibited in
this Gospel, and then, by teaching them that it is not a sin
to kill men by the command of the authorities, but that it is

a sin not to obey the authorities, and so forth.

Thus the deception of the soldiers, which consists in this, that they are impressed with the idea that it is possible without sinning to kill men by command of the authorities, does not stand alone, but is connected with a whole system of deceptions, without which this particular deception would be ineffective.

Only a man who is completely stupefied by that false faith, called Orthodox, which is given out to him as being Christian, is able to believe that it is no sin for a Christian to enter the army, promising blindly to obey any man who will consider himself higher in rank, and, at the command of another man, to learn to kill and to commit this most terrible crime, which is prohibited by all the laws.

A man who is free from the deception of the so-called Orthodox, pseudo-Christian faith will never believe this.

For this reason the so-called sectarians, that is, the Christians who reject the doctrine of Orthodoxy and acknowledge Christ's teaching, as it is expounded in the Gospels, and especially in the Sermon on the Mount, never fall a prey to this deception, and have always refused to do military service, recognizing it as incompatible with Christianity and preferring to suffer all kinds of tortures, as is now done by hundreds and thousands of men,—in Russia by the Dukhobors and Milkers; in Austria by the Nazarenes; in Sweden, Switzerland, and Germany by the Evangelists. The government knows this and so follows nothing with such terror and attention as that the general ecclesiastic deception, without which its power is not possible, shall be practiced from earliest childhood on all the children and shall be constantly maintained in such a way that not one man can escape it. The government permits anything, drunkenness and debauchery (it not only permits, but even encourages drunkenness and debauchery,—it helps in the stultification), but it is violently opposed to allowing men to free themselves from the deception and free others from it.

The Russian government practices this deception with particular cruelty and harshness. It commands all its subjects, threatening them with punishment in case of non-compliance, to have all their children baptized, while they are babes, into the deceptive, so-called Orthodox faith. When the children are baptized, that is, are considered Orthodox, they are, under threat of criminal prosecution, prohibited from discussing the faith into which they were baptized without their will, and for such a discussion of the faith, as well as for departing from it and passing over to another faith, they are subject to punishments.

So it cannot be said of all the Russians that they believe in the Orthodox faith,—they do not know whether they believe or not, because they were turned into that faith when they were still babes, and because they hold to this enforced faith through fear of punishment. All the Russians are caught into Orthodoxy through fell deception and are kept in it through cruel violence.

By making use of the power which it has, the government produces and maintains the deception, and the deception maintains its power.

And so the only means for freeing men from all the calamities consists in freeing them from that false faith which is inculcated upon them by the government, and in impressing upon them the true Christian teaching, which is concealed from them by this false doctrine. The true Christian teaching is very simple, clear, and accessible, as Christ Himself has said. But it is simple and accessible only when a man is free from that lie in which we are all brought up, and which is given out to us as divine.

It is impossible to fill a vessel with what is important, if it is already filled with what is useless. It is necessary first to pour out what is useless. Even so it is with the acquisition of the true Christian teaching. We must first understand that all the stories about how God created the world six thousand years ago, and how Adam sinned, and how the human race fell, and how the son of God and God Himself, born of a virgin, came into the world and redeemed it, and all the fables of the Bible and of the Gospel, and all the lives of the saints, and the stories of miracles and relics, are nothing but a coarse mixing up of the superstitions of the Jewish nation with the deceptions of the clergy. Only for a man who is completely free from these deceptions can the simple and clear teaching of Christ, which demands no interpretations and is self-comprehensible, be accessible and comprehensible.

This teaching says nothing about the beginning or the end of the world, nor of God and His intentions, in general nothing about what we cannot know and need not know, but speaks only of what a man has to do in order to be saved, that is, in order in the best manner possible to pass the life into which he has come in this world, from his birth to his death. For this purpose we need only treat others as we wish to be treated. In this alone does the law and the prophets consist, as Christ has said. To do so, we need no images, no relics, no divine services, no priests, no sacred histories, no catechisms, no governments, but, on the contrary, a liberation from all that—because only the man who is free from those fables which the priests give out to him as the only truth, and who is not bound to other people by promises to act as they want him to act, can treat others as he wishes to be treated by them. Only in that case will a man be able to do, not his own will, nor that of others, but the will of God.

But the will of God consists, not in fighting and oppressing others, but in recognizing all men as brothers and serving one another.

Such are the thoughts that your letter evoked in me. I shall be very glad if they shall contribute to the elucidation of the questions in which you are interested.

"THE SOLDIERS' MEMENTO"

(1901)

You are a soldier, you have been taught to shoot, stab, march, go through gymnastic exercises, read books, and have been taken out to military exercises and parades; maybe you went through a war, fighting the Turks or the Chinese, doing everything you were commanded to do. It did not even occur to you to ask yourself whether what you were doing was good or bad.

But here the command is given to your company or squadron to start out, taking along ball-cartridges. You travel or march, without asking whither you are taken.

You are led up to a village or factory, and you see from afar that in the open square there is a crowd of villagers or factory hands, men, women with their children, old men and women. The governor and the prosecutor, accompanied by policemen, walk up to the crowd and talk to the people about something. The crowd is at first silent, then the people begin to cry out louder and louder, and the officials go away from the crowd. You see that these are peasants or factory hands who are riotous, and that you are brought there to pacify them. The officials several times walk up to the people and walk away again, but the shouts grow louder and louder, and the officials talk among themselves, and you are commanded to load your gun with a ball-cartridge. You see before yourself people, the same from among whom you were taken: men in sleeveless coats, short fur coats, bast shoes, and women in kerchiefs and waists, just such women as your wife or mother.

The first shot you are ordered to fire above the heads of

the crowd; but the people do not disperse, and shout louder than before. Then you are commanded to shoot right, not over their heads, but straight into the crowd.

You have been impressed with the idea that you are not responsible for what will happen from your shot; but you know that the man who, weltering in blood, fell down from your shot was killed by you and by no one else, and you know that you might not have shot, and then the man would not have been killed.

What are you to do?

It is not enough for you to drop your gun and refuse just now to shoot at your brothers. To-morrow the same may be repeated, and, so, whether you wish it or not, you must bethink yourself and ask yourself what this calling of a soldier is, which has brought you to such a state that you are compelled to shoot at your own unarmed brothers.

In the Gospel it says that we must not only not kill our brothers, but must also not do what leads to murder, that we must not be angry with our brother, and that we must not hate our enemies, but love them.

In the law of Moses it says distinctly, "Thou shalt not kill," without any explanations as to who may be killed and who not. But in the rules which you have been taught it says that a soldier must fulfil any command of his superior, no matter what it may be, except a command against the Tsar, and in the explanation of the sixth commandment it says that, though the commandment forbids killing, he who kills in war does not sin against this commandment.[1] But in the *Soldiers' Memento*, which hangs in every barrack and which you have read and heard many a time, it says that a soldier must kill men: "Three fly at you,—the first you stab, the second you shoot, the third you settle with the bayonet . . . if the bayonet is broken, beat with the butt;

[1] In the Rules it says: "By the sixth commandment God forbids us to take the lives of men by violence or cunning, or in any way to violate the security and peace of our neighbour, and so by this commandment quarrels, anger, hatred, envy, and cruelty are also forbidden. But he who kills the enemy in war does not sin against this commandment, because by war he defends our faith, our Tsar, and our country."—*Author's Note*.

if the butt won't do, belabour him with your fists; if your fists give out, hang to him with your teeth."[1]

You are told that you must kill, because you have taken the oath, and that the authorities, and not you, will be responsible for your acts.

But before you swore, that is, promised people to do their will, you were even without an oath obliged in everything to do the will of God, of Him who gave you life,—but God has commanded us not to kill.

Thus you could not swear that you would do *everything* demanded of you by men. For this reason it says directly in the Gospel (Matt. v. 34), "Swear not at all" . . . "But let your communication be, Yea, yea; Nay, nay: for whatsoever is more than these cometh of evil." And the same is said in James v. 12: "But above all things, my brethren, swear not, neither by heaven, neither by earth," etc. Thus the oath itself is a sin. And what they say to the effect that not you, but the authorities, will be responsible for your acts is an untruth. Can your conscience be, not in yourself, but in the corporal, sergeant, captain, colonel, or anybody else? Nobody can decide for you what you can and must do, and what you cannot and must not do. A man is always responsible for what he does. Is not the sin of adultery many times lighter than the sin of murder, and can a man say to another, "Commit adultery, I take your sin upon myself, because I am your superior"?

Adam, so the Bible tells, sinned against God and then said that his wife had told him to eat the apple, that the devil had tempted her. God justified neither Adam nor Eve, and told them that Adam would be punished for having listened to the voice of his wife, and that his wife would be likewise punished for having obeyed the serpent. He did not free them, but punished them. Will not God say the same to you, when you kill a man and say that your captain commanded you to do so?

---

[1] *Soldiers' Memento,* collected by Dragomírov, 19th ed., St. Petersburg, 1899.

The deception is seen even in this, that in the rule which says that a soldier must fulfil all the commandments of his superiors, the words are added: "Except such as are to the harm of the Tsar."

If a soldier, before fulfilling the commands of his superior, must decide whether they are not against the Tsar, how much more must he, before fulfilling the command of his superior, consider whether what his officer demands of him is not against the highest Tsar, God! But there is no act which is more opposed to God's will than the killing of men. And so it is not right to obey men, if they command you to kill men. But if you obey and kill, you do so only for your advantage, in order not to be punished. Thus, by killing by the command of your superiors, you are as much a murderer as that robber who kills a merchant, in order to rob him. The robber is tempted by the money, and you are tempted by the desire not to be punished and to receive a reward. A man always himself answers for his acts before God.

No power can, as the authorities want it to, make of you, of a living man, a dead thing which may be handled as desired. Christ has taught men that they are all sons of God, and so a Christian cannot give his conscience into the power of another man, no matter by what title he may be called,— king, Tsar, or emperor. The fact that the men who have taken the command over you demand of you that you shall kill your brothers, proves only that these men are cheats and that, therefore, you must not obey them. Shameful is the position of the harlot who is always prepared to have her body defiled by him who is pointed out to her by her master; but more shameful is the position of the soldier who is always prepared to commit the greatest crime,— to murder any man who is pointed out to him by his superior.

And so, if you really want to act in godly fashion, you must do this: you must give up the disgraceful and godless calling of a soldier and be prepared to bear all the sufferings which they will impose upon you for this.

Thus the real memento of a Christian soldier is not the one

in which it says that "God is the soldiers' general," and other blasphemies, and that "a soldier must, while obeying his superiors in everything, be prepared to kill strangers or friends, even his unarmed brothers;" he must remember the words of Scripture that God must be obeyed more than men, and he must not fear those who can kill the body, but cannot kill the soul.

In this consists the true soldiers' memento, which does not deceive.

Gáspra, December 7, 1901.

"THE OFFICERS' MEMENTO"

(1901)

In all soldier quarters there hangs upon the wall a so-called *Soldiers' Memento,* composed by General Dragomírov. This *Memento* is a conglomeration of stupid, slangy, supposedly popular words (though they are quite foreign to any soldier), mixed with blasphemous quotations from the Gospel. Gospel sayings are adduced in confirmation of the statement that the soldiers must kill and chew their enemies: "If the bayonet is broken, fight with your fists; if your fists give out, hang on with your teeth." At the end of the *Memento* it says that God is the soldiers' general.

Nothing proves more conclusively than this *Memento* to what a terrible degree of ignorance, slavish obedience, and bestiality our Russians have come. Ever since this most terrible blasphemy has made its appearance and was hung up in all the barracks,— and this was done very long ago,— not one chief, not one priest, who, one would think, would directly be affected by the distortion of the meaning of the Gospel texts, has expressed his condemnation of this disgusting production, and it continues to be printed in millions of copies and to be read by millions of soldiers, who accept this terrible work as a guide in their activity.

This *Memento* long ago roused my indignation, and now, fearing that I shall not be able to do so again, before my death, I have written an address to the soldiers, in which I try to remind them that, as men and Christians, they have quite different obligations before God than those which are put forth in this *Memento*. Such a reminder, I think, is not only necessary for the soldiers, but to an even greater degree for the officerdom (by officerdom I mean all the military authorities, from the ensign to the general), which enters military service or remains in it, not from compulsion, like the soldiers, but from choice. This reminder, it seems to me, is particularly needed in our time.

It was all very well one hundred or fifty years ago, when war was considered to be an inevitable condition of the life of nations, when the men belonging to the nation with which war was waged were considered barbarians, infidels, or malefactors, and when it did not even occur to the military that they would be needed for the suppression and pacification of their own nations,—it was all very well then for a man to put on a bright-coloured, lace-covered uniform, to walk, causing the sabre to rattle and the spurs to tinkle, or to let his horse go through evolutions in front of the regiment, imagining that he was a hero, who, if he had not yet sacrificed, was prepared to sacrifice his life in the defense of his country. But now, when the frequent international relations—mercantile, social, scientific, artistic—have so brought the nations together that any war among the modern nations presents itself in the form of a family dissension which violates the most sacred ties of men; when hundreds of peace societies and thousands of articles, not only in special periodicals, but also in the general newspapers, never cease in every manner possible to make clear the madness of militarism and the possibility, even the necessity, of abolishing war; when, and this is the most important thing of all, the military have more and more frequently to proceed, not against a foreign enemy, in order to defend the country against attacking conquerors or to increase the country's glory and power, but against unarmed factory hands and peasants,— the galloping on a steed, in a lace-bedecked uniform, and the dandyish appearance in front of the company no longer is a case of trifling, pardonable ambition, which it used to be formerly, but something quite different.

In olden times, say in the days of Nicholas I., it never as much as occurred to any one that the armies were needed preëminently for the purpose of shooting unarmed citizens. But now troops are regularly quartered in the capitals and manufacturing centres, so as to be ready to disperse working men, and hardly a month passes but that the troops are taken out of their barracks with their ball-cartridges and are located in a protected place, ready at any moment to shoot at the masses.

The use of the army against the masses has not only become a customary phenomenon, but the troops are in advance formed in such a way as to be ready for such emergencies. The government does not conceal the fact that the distribution of recruits according to districts is intentionally made in such a way that the soldiers are never drafted from the localities where they are quartered. This is done so as to avoid the necessity of having the soldiers shoot at their own parents.

The Emperor of Germany has said plainly at every levy of recruits (his speech of May 23, 1901) that the soldiers swearing allegiance to him belong to him, body and soul, and that they have but one enemy, and that is, his enemy, and that his enemies are the socialists (that is, the working people), whom the soldiers must, if commanded, shoot down ("*niederschiessen*"), even though these be their own brothers or even parents.

Besides, if in former times the troops were used against the masses, those against whom they were used were, or at least were supposed to be, malefactors, ready to ruin and kill peaceful citizens, who, therefore, had to be destroyed for the common good. But now everybody knows that those against whom the troops are sent out are for the most part peaceable, industrious people, who merely desire without interference to enjoy the fruits of their labours. Thus the chief and constant use of troops in our time no longer consists in an imaginary defense against infidel and in general foreign enemies, nor against riotous malefactors, domestic enemies, but in killing their unarmed brothers, who are not all malefactors, but peaceable, industrious people, who only do not wish to have what they earn taken away from them. Thus military service in our time, when its chief purpose is by the threat of killing and by murder itself to retain the enslaved people in those unjust conditions in which they are, is no longer a noble, but a despicable business.

And so it is necessary for the officers who are now serving to think about whom they are serving, and to ask themselves whether what they are doing is good or bad.

I know there are many officers, especially among the higher ranks, who by all kinds of reflections on the subject of Orthodoxy, autocracy, integrity of the state, the inevitableness of imminent war, the need of order, the senselessness of the socialistic ravings, and so forth, try to prove to themselves that their activity is rational and useful, and has nothing immoral about it. But in the depth of their hearts they themselves do not believe in what they say, and the more sensible and the older they are, the less do they believe in it.

I remember how pleasantly I was surprised by my friend and comrade in the service, a very ambitious man, who had devoted all his life to military service and had attained the highest ranks and distinctions (he was an adjutant-general and a general of artillery), when he told me that he had burned his memoirs on the wars in which he had taken part, because he had changed his view on military matters and now considered every war a bad business, which ought not to be encouraged by busying oneself with it, but, on the contrary, ought in every way possible to be discredited. Many officers believe the same thing, though they do not say so, while they serve. In fact, no thinking officer can think differently. We need but think what, beginning with the lowest ranks and ending with the highest, that of a commander of a corps, constitutes the occupation of all the officers. From the beginning to the end of their service,—I am speaking of the officers in active service,—their activity, with the exception of rare, short periods, when they go to war and are busy with murder, consists in the attainment of two ends,—

in instructing the soldiers in the best possible way to kill men and in teaching them such obedience that they will be able mechanically, without any reflection, to do what their chief may demand of them. In olden times they used to say, "flog two unmercifully and get one well instructed," and so they did. If now the percentage of flogged is less, the principle remains the same. People cannot be brought to that animal and even mechanical condition, when they will do what is most repugnant to their natures and the faith professed by them, namely, murder, at the command of any superior, unless not only cunning deception but even most cruel violence has been practiced against them. And so it is done.

Lately a great sensation was created in the French press by the disclosure of some journalists as to the terrible tortures practiced on the soldiers of the disciplinary battalions in the island of Obrou, within six hours' travel from Paris. The persons punished had their arms and legs tied together behind their backs and were thrown on the floor, screws were put on the thumbs of the hands, which were bent behind their backs, and these screws were so tightened that every motion produced excruciating pain, men were suspended by their legs, and so forth.

When we see trained animals performing what is contrary to their natures,—dogs walking on their fore legs, elephants whirling barrels, tigers playing with lions, and so forth,—we know that all this has been obtained by tortures, by means of hunger, the whip, and the hot iron. We know the same when we see men, in uniforms and with their guns, stand stark still, or go through the same motion with absolute regularity, run, jump, shoot, shout, and so forth, in general execute those beautiful parades and manœuvres, which the emperors and kings admire so much and brag of to one another. It is impossible to drive everything human out of a man and to bring him to the condition of a machine, without torturing him, not in a simple way, but in the most refined and cruel manner, both torturing and deceiving him.

All this you officers do. In this, with the rare exceptions

when you go to war, does your service, from the highest to the lowest ranks, consist.

To you comes a youth who is taken away from his family and is settled at the opposite end of the world, and who is impressed with the idea that the deceptive oath, forbidden by the Gospel, which he has taken, binds him irretrievably, just as a cock placed on the floor, on which a chalk-line is drawn from his beak, imagines that he is tied with this line. He comes to you with full humility and with the hope that you, the elders, who are wiser and more learned than he, will teach him everything that is good. But you, instead of freeing him from those superstitions which he has brought with him, inoculate in him new, most senseless, coarse, and harmful superstitions: about the sacredness of the flag, the almost divine significance of the Tsar, the duty of submitting without a murmur to the authorities. When, with the aid of methods worked out in your business for the stultification of men, you bring him to a condition worse than that of an animal, in which he is ready to kill anybody he is commanded to kill, even his unarmed brothers, you proudly show him to the higher power and receive thanks and rewards for this. It is terrible for a man to be a murderer himself, but by means of cunning and cruel methods to bring to this his brothers who confide in him is a most terrible crime. And this you are committing, and in this does your service consist.

So it is not surprising that among you, more than in any other circle, flourish all those things which can drown conscience,—smoking, cards, drunkenness, debauchery,—and that more frequently than anywhere else occur suicides.

"It must be that offenses come into the world; but woe to them by whom the offenses come."

You frequently say that you serve, because, if you did not serve, the existing order would be impaired and there would be disorder and all kinds of calamities.

But, in the first place, it is not true that you are concerned about the maintenance of the existing order: you are only concerned about your personal advantage.

In the second place, even if your refraining from doing military service should impair the existing order, this would not at all prove that you must continue to do what is bad, but only that the order which will be destroyed through your abstinence ought to be destroyed. Even if there existed the most useful institutions, such as hospitals, schools, homes for the aged, which would be maintained from the revenue derived from houses of prostitution, all the usefulness of these charitable institutions could not keep in her condition a woman who should wish to free herself from her disgraceful calling.

"It is not my fault," the woman would say, "that you have established your charitable institutions on debauchery. I do not want to be a harlot, and with your institutions I have nothing to do." The same ought to be said by every military man, when he is told of the necessity of maintaining the existing order, which is based on the readiness to commit murder. "Establish a general order, such that murder will not be necessary for it," is what a military man should say, "and I will not violate it. I simply do not want to be a murderer."

Many others of you say: "I was educated that way, I am fettered by my position, and I cannot get out of it." But even that is not true.

You can always get out of your position. If you do not, it is because you prefer to live and act against your conscience, rather than lose some of the worldly advantages which you derive from your dishonourable calling. Only forget that you are officers and remember that you are men, and the way out from your condition will at once present itself to you. This way out, the best and most honourable, consists in this, that you call together the part which you command, step to the front, beg the soldiers' pardon for the wrong which you have done them by deceiving them, and stop being a military man. This act seems very bold and seems to call for much courage; and yet, much less courage is needed in this act than in storming a fort or challenging to a duel for an insult to your uniform,—what you are always ready to do and always do in your capacity as a military man.

But even if you are not able to act in this manner, you are still able, if you have come to understand the criminality of military service, to leave that service and prefer any other activity to it, even though it be less advantageous.

But if you are not able to do even that, the solution of the question as to whether you will continue to serve will be put off for you until the time—and this time will soon arrive for everybody—when you shall stand face to face with an unarmed crowd of peasants or factory hands, and you shall be commanded to shoot at them. And then if any human feeling is left in you, you will be compelled to refuse to obey and in consequence of this will certainly leave the service.

I know there are many officers still, from the highest to the lowest ranks, who are so ignorant or so hypnotized that they do not see the necessity of any of these three conclusions, and calmly continue to serve and under the present conditions are prepared to shoot at their brothers and are even proud of the fact; fortunately, public opinion more and more punishes these men with contempt and loathing, and their number is growing less and less.

Thus in our time, when the fratricidal purpose of the army has become obvious, it is impossible for the officers to continue the ancient traditions of the military self-satisfied bravado; they cannot even, without recognizing their human degradation and shame, continue the criminal business of teaching simple people who have faith in them how to commit murder, and themselves be ready to take part in the murder of unarmed men.

It is this that every thinking and conscientious officer of our time should understand and remember.

Gáspra, December 7, 1901.

PATRIOTISM OR PEACE

LETTER TO MANSON

(1896)

DEAR SIR:—You write to me asking me to express myself in respect to the United States of North America "in the interests of Christian consistency and true peace," and express the hope that "the nations will soon awaken to the one means of securing national peace."

I harbour the same hope. I harbour the same hope, because the blindness in our time of the nations that extol patriotism, bring up their young generations in the superstition of patriotism, and, at the same time, do not wish for the inevitable consequences of patriotism,—war,—has, it seems to me, reached such a last stage that the simplest reflection, which begs for utterance in the mouth of every unprejudiced man, is sufficient, in order that men may see the crying contradiction in which they are.

Frequently, when you ask children which they will choose of two things which are incompatible, but which they want alike, they answer, "Both."

"Which do you want,—to go out driving or to stay at home?"—"Both,—go out driving and stay at home."

Just so the Christian nations answer the question which life puts to them, as to which they will choose, patriotism or peace, they answer "Both patriotism and peace," though it is as impossible to unite patriotism with peace, as at the same time to go out driving and stay at home.

The other day there arose a difference between the United States and England concerning the borders of Venezuela.

Salisbury for some reason did not agree to something; Cleveland wrote a message to the Senate; from either side were raised patriotic warlike cries; a panic ensued upon 'Change; people lost millions of pounds and of dollars; Edison announced that he would invent engines with which it would be possible to kill more men in an hour than Atilla had killed in all his wars, and both nations began energetically to arm themselves for war. But because, simultaneously with these preparations for war, both in England and in America, all kinds of literary men, princes, and statesmen began to admonish their respective governments to abstain from war, saying that the subject under discussion was not sufficiently important to begin a war for, especially between two related Anglo-Saxon nations, speaking the same language, who ought not to war among themselves, but ought calmly to govern others; or because all kinds of bishops, archdeacons, canons prayed and preached concerning the matter in all the churches; or because neither side considered itself sufficiently prepared,— it happened that there was no war just then. And people calmed down.

But a person has to have too little perspicacity not to see that the causes which now are leading to a conflict between England and America have remained the same, and that, if even the present conflict shall be settled without a war, there will inevitably to-morrow or the day after appear other conflicts, between England and Russia, between England and Turkey, in all possible permutations, as they arise every day, and one of these will lead to war.

If two armed men live side by side, having been impressed from childhood with the idea that power, wealth, and glory are the highest virtues, and that, therefore, to acquire power, wealth, and glory by means of arms, to the detriment of other neighbouring possessors, is a very praiseworthy matter, and if at the same time there is no moral, religious, or political restraint for these men, is it not evident that such people will always fight, that the normal relation between them will be war? and that, if such people, having clutched one another, have separated for awhile, they have done so only, as the French proverb says, *"pour mieux sauter,"* that is, they have separated to take a better run, to throw themselves with greater fury upon one another?

Strange is the egotism of private individuals, but the egotists of private life are not armed, do not consider it right either to prepare or use arms against their adversaries; the egotism of private individuals is under the control of the political power and of public opinion. A private person who with gun in his hand takes away his neighbour's cow, or a desyatína of his crop, will immediately be seized by a policeman and put into prison. Besides, such a man will be condemned by public opinion,—he will be called a thief and robber. It is quite different with the states: they are all armed,—there is no power over them, except the comical attempts at catching a bird by pouring some salt on its tail,—attempts at establishing international congresses, which, apparently, will never be accepted by the powerful states (who are armed for the very purpose that they may not pay any attention to any one), and, above all, public opinion, which rebukes every act of violence in a private individual, extols, raises to the virtue of patriotism every appropriation of what belong to others, for the increase of the power of the country.

Open the newspapers for any period you may wish, and at any moment you will see the black spot,—the cause of every possible war: now it is Korea, now the Pamir, now the lands in Africa, now Abyssinia, now Turkey, now Venezuela, now the Transvaal. The work of the robbers does not stop for a moment, and here and there a small war, like an exchange of shots in the cordon, is going on all the time, and the real war can and will begin at any moment.

If an American wishes the preferential grandeur and well-being of America above all other nations, and the same is desired for his state by an Englishman, and a Russian, and a Turk, and a Dutchman, and an Abyssinian, and a citizen of Venezuela and of the Transvaal, and an Armenian, and a Pole, and a Bohemian, and all of them are convinced that these desires need not only not be concealed or repressed, but should be a matter of pride and be developed in themselves and in others; and if the greatness and well-being of one country or nation cannot be obtained except to the detriment of another nation, frequently of many countries and nations,—how can war be avoided?

And so, not to have any war, it is not necessary to preach and pray to God about peace, to persuade the English-speaking nations that they ought to be friendly toward one another, in order to be able to rule over other nations; to form double and triple alliances against one another; to marry princes to princesses of other nations,—but to destroy what produces war. But what produces war is the desire for an exclusive good for one's own nation,—what is called patriotism. And so to abolish war, it is necessary to abolish patriotism, and to abolish patriotism, it is necessary first to become convinced that it is an evil, and that it is hard to do. Tell people that war is bad, and they will laugh at you: who does not know that? Tell them that patriotism is bad, and the majority of people will agree with you, but with a small proviso. "Yes, bad patriotism is bad, but there is also another patriotism, the one we adhere to." But wherein this good patriotism consists no one can explain. If good patriotism consists in not being acquisitive, as many say, it is none the less retentive; that is, men want to retain what was formerly acquired, since there is no country which was not based on conquest, and it is impossible to retain what is conquered by any other means than those by which it was acquired, that is, by violence and murder. But even if patriotism is not retentive, it is restorative,—the patriotism of the vanquished and oppressed nations, the Armenians, Poles, Bohemians, Irish, and so forth. This patriotism is almost the very worst, because it is the most enraged and demands the greatest degree of violence.

Patriotism cannot be good. Why do not people say that egotism can be good, though this may be asserted more easily, because egotism is a natural sentiment, with which a man is born, while patriotism is an unnatural sentiment, which is artificially inoculated in him?

It will be said: "Patriotism has united men in states and keeps up the unity of the states." But the men are already united in states,—the work is all done: why should men now maintain an exclusive loyalty for their state, when this loyalty produces calamities for all states and nations? The same patriotism which produced the unification of men into states is now destroying those states. If there were but one patriotism,—the patriotism of none but the English,—it might be regarded as unificatory or beneficent, but when, as now, there are American, English, German, French, Russian patriotisms, all of them opposed to one another, patriotism no longer unites, but disunites. To say that, if patriotism was beneficent, by uniting men into states, as was the case during its highest development in Greece and Rome, patriotism even now, after eighteen hundred years of Christian life, is just as beneficent, is the same as saying that, since the ploughing was useful and beneficent for the field before the sowing, it will be as useful now, after the crop has grown up.

It would be very well to retain patriotism in memory of the use which it once had, as people preserve and retain the ancient monuments of temples, mausoleums, and so forth. But the temples and mausoleums stand, without causing any harm to men, while patriotism produces without cessation innumerable calamities.

What now causes the Armenians and the Turks to suffer and cut each other's throats and act like wild beasts? Why do England and Russia, each of them concerned about her share of the inheritance from Turkey, lie in wait and do not put a stop to the Armenian atrocities? Why do the Abyssinians and Italians fight one another? Why did a terrible war come very near breaking out on account of Venezuela, and now on account of the Transvaal? And the Chino-Japanese War, and the Turkish, and the German, and the French wars? And the rage of the subdued nations, the Armenians, the Poles, the Irish? And the preparation for war by all the nations? All that is the fruits of patriotism. Seas of blood have been shed for the sake of this sentiment, and more blood will be shed for its sake, if men do not free themselves from this outlived bit of antiquity.

I have several times had occasion to write about patriotism, about its absolute incompatibility, not only with the teaching of Christ in its ideal sense, but even with the lowest demands of the morality of Christian society, and every time my arguments have been met with silence or with the supercilious hint that the ideas expressed by me were Utopian expressions of mysticism, anarchism, and cosmopolitanism. My ideas have frequently been repeated in a compressed form, and, instead of retorting to them, it was added that it was nothing but cosmopolitanism, as though this word "cosmopolitanism" unanswerably overthrew all my arguments. Serious, old, clever, good men, who, above all else, stand like the city on a hill, and who involuntarily guide the masses by their example, make it appear that the legality and beneficence of patriotism are so obvious and incontestable that it is not worth while to answer the frivolous and senseless attacks upon this sentiment, and the majority of men, who have since childhood been deceived and infected by patriotism, take this supercilious silence to be a most convincing proof, and continue to stick fast in their ignorance.

And so those people who from their position can free the masses from their calamities, and do not do so, commit a great sin.

The most terrible thing in world is hypocrisy. There was good reason why Christ once got angry,—that was against the hypocrisy of the Pharisees.

But what was the hypocrisy of the Pharisees in comparison with the hypocrisy of our time? In comparison with our men, the Pharisees were the most truthful of men, and their art of hypocrisy was as child's play in comparison with the hypocrisy of our time; nor can it be otherwise. Our whole life, with the profession of Christianity, the teaching of humility and love, in connection with the life of an armed den of robbers, can be nothing but one solid, terrible hypocrisy. It is very convenient to profess a teaching at one end of which is Christian sanctity and infallibility, and at the other—the pagan sword and gallows, so that, when it is possible to impose or deceive by means of sanctity, sanctity is put into effect, and when the deception does not work, the sword and the gallows are put into effect. Such a teaching is very convenient, but the time comes when this spider-web of lie is dispersed, and it is no longer possible to continue to keep both, and it is necessary to ally oneself with either one or the other. It is this which is now getting to be the case in relation to the teaching about patriotism.

Whether people want it or not, the question stands clearly before humanity: how can that patriotism, from which result innumerable physical and moral calamities of men, be necessary and a virtue? It is indispensable to give an answer to this question.

It is necessary either to show that patriotism is such a great good that it redeems all those terrible calamities which it produces in humanity; or to recognize that patriotism is an evil, which must not only not be inoculated in men and impressed upon them, but from which also we must try to free ourselves at all cost.

C'est à prendre ou à laisser, as the French say. If patriotism is good, then Christianity, which gives peace, is an idle dream, and the sooner this teaching is eradicated, the better. But if Christianity really gives peace, and we really want peace, patriotism is a survival from barbarous times, which must not only not be evoked and educated, as we now do, but which must be eradicated by all means, by preaching, persuasion, contempt, and ridicule. If Christianity is the truth, and we wish to live in peace, we must not only have no sympathy for the power of our country, but must even rejoice in its weakening, and contribute to it. A Russian must rejoice when Poland, the Baltic provinces, Finland, Armenia, are separated from Russia and made free; and an Englishman must similarly rejoice in relation to Ireland, Australia, India, and the other colonies, and coöperate in it, because, the greater the country, the more evil and cruel is its patriotism, and the greater is the amount of the suffering on which its power is based. And so, if we actually want to be what we profess, we must not, as we do now, wish for the increase of our country, but wish for its diminution and weakening, and contribute to it with all our means. And thus must we educate the younger generations: we must bring up the younger generations in such a way that, as it is now disgraceful for a young man to manifest his coarse egotism, for example, by eating everything up, without leaving anything for others, to push a weaker person down from the road, in order to pass by himself, to take away by force what another needs, it should be just as disgraceful to wish for the increase of his country's power; and, as it now is considered stupid and ridiculous for a person to praise himself, it should be considered stupid to extol one's nations, as is now done in various lying patriotic histories, pictures, monuments, textbooks, articles, sermons, and stupid national hymns. But it must be understood that so long as we are going to extol patriotism and educate the younger generations in it, we shall have armaments, which ruin the physical and spiritual life of the nations, and wars, terrible, horrible wars, like those for which we are preparing ourselves, and into the circle of which we are introducing, corrupting them with our patriotism, the new, terrible fighters of the distant East.

Emperor William, one of the most comical persons of our time, orator, poet, musician, dramatic writer, and artist, and, above all, patriot, has lately painted a picture representing all the nations of Europe with swords, standing at the seashore, and, at the indication of Archangel Michael, looking at the sitting figures of Buddha and Confucius in the distance. According to William's intention, this should mean that the nations of Europe ought to unite in order to defend themselves against the peril which is proceeding from there. He is quite right from his coarse, pagan, patriotic point of view, which is eighteen hundred years behind the times. The European nations, forgetting Christ, have in the name of their patriotism more and more irritated these peaceful nations, and have taught them patriotism and war, and have now irritated them so much that, indeed, if Japan and China will as fully forget the teachings of Buddha and of Confucius as we have forgotten the teachings of Christ, they will soon learn the art of killing people (they learn these things quickly, as Japan has proved), and, being fearless, agile, strong, and populous, they will inevitably very soon make of the countries of Europe, if Europe does not invent something stronger than guns and Edison's inventions, what the countries of Europe are making of Africa. "The disciple is not above his master but every one that is perfect shall be as his master" (Luke vi. 40).

In reply to a prince's question how to increase his army, in order to conquer a southern tribe which did not submit to him, Confucius replied: "Destroy all thy army, and use the money, which thou art wasting now on the army, on the enlightenment of thy people and on the improvement of agriculture, and the southern tribe will drive away its prince and will submit to thy rule without war."

Thus taught Confucius, whom we are advised to fear. But we, having forgotten Christ's teaching, having renounced it, wish to vanquish the nations by force, and thus are only preparing for ourselves new and stronger enemies than our neighbours. A friend of mine, who saw William's picture, said: "The picture is beautiful, only it does not at all represent what the legend says. It means that Archangel Michael shows to all the governments of Europe, which are represented as robbers bedecked with arms, what it is that will cause their ruin and annihilation, namely, the meekness of Buddha and the wisdom of Confucius." He might have added, "And the humility of Lao-tse."

Indeed, we, thanks to our hypocrisy, have forgotten Christ to such an extent, have so squeezed out of our life everything Christian, that the teachings of Buddha and Confucius stand incomparably higher than that beastly patriotism, by which our so-called Christian nations are guided. And so the salvation of Europe and of the Christian world at large does not consist in this, that, bedecking themselves with swords, as William has represented them, they should, like robbers, cast themselves upon their brothers beyond the sea, in order to kill them, but, on the contrary, they should renounce the survival of barbarous times,—patriotism,—and, having renounced it, should take off their arms and show the Eastern nations, not an example of savage patriotism and beastliness, but an example of brotherly love, which Christ has taught us.

Moscow, January 2, 1896.

PATRIOTISM AND GOVERNMENT

(1900)

I

I HAVE several times had occasion to express the idea that patriotism is in our time an unnatural, irrational, harmful sentiment, which causes the greater part of those calamities from which humanity suffers, and that, therefore, this sentiment ought not to be cultivated, as it now is, but, on the contrary, ought to be repressed and destroyed with all means that sensible people can command. But, strange to say, in spite of the evident and incontestable relation of the universal armaments and destructive wars, which ruin the nations, to this exclusive sentiment, all my arguments as to the obsoleteness, untimeliness, and harm of patriotism have been met either with silence or with intentional misunderstanding, or, again, with the same strange retort: "What is said is that there is harm in the bad patriotism, jingoism, chauvinism, but the real, good patriotism is a very elevated, moral sentiment, which it is not only senseless, but even criminal to condemn." But as to what this real, good patriotism consists in, either nothing is said, or, instead of an explanation, they utter pompous, highfalutin phrases, or something which has nothing in common with patriotism is put in the place of this patriotism, which we all know and from which we suffer so cruelly.

They generally say that the true, good patriotism consists in wishing the real good for one's nation or state, the good which does not impair that of the other nations.

The other day, while speaking with an Englishman about

the present war, I told him that the real cause was not any selfish aims, as is generally assumed, but patriotism, as was evident from the mood of all English society. The Englishman did not agree with me, and said that if that was true, it was due to the fact that the patriotism which was now animating the English was a false patriotism, but that the good patriotism, with which he was permeated, consisted in this, that the English, his fellow citizens, should not act badly.

"Do you wish that only the English should not act badly?" I asked.

"I wish this to all!" he answered, showing plainly by this answer that the properties of benefits—be they moral, scientific, or even applied, practical—are by their nature such that they extend over all men, and so the desire for such benefits for any one is not only no patriotism, but even excludes it.

Similarly the peculiarities of every nation, which some other defenders of patriotism intentionally substitute for this concept, are no patriotism. They say that the peculiarities of each nation constitute an indispensable condition for the progress of humanity, and so patriotism, which strives after the retention of these peculiarities, is a good and useful sentiment. But is it not obvious that if at some time the peculiarities of each nation, its customs, beliefs, language formed an indispensable condition of the life of humanity, these same peculiarities serve in our time as the chief impediment to the realization of the ideal of the brotherly union of the nations, which is already cognized by men? And so the maintenance and preservation of the peculiarities of any nationality, Russian, German, French, Anglo-Saxon, provoking a similar maintenance and preservation not only on the part of the Hungarian, Polish, Irish nationalities, but also on the part of the Basque, Provençal, Mordvinian, Chuvash, and a mass of other nationalities, does not make for the closer friendship and union of men, but for their greater and ever greater estrangement and division.

Thus it is not the imaginary, but the real patriotism, the

one which we all know, under the influence of which the majority of the men of our time are, and from which humanity is suffering so cruelly, that is, not a desire for spiritual benefits for one's nation (it is impossible to wish for spiritual benefits for only one's own nation), and not the peculiarities of national individualities (that is a quality, and by no means a sentiment), but a very definite feeling of preferring one's own nation or state to all the other nations and states, and so it is a desire that this nation or state enjoy the greatest welfare and .greatness, which can be obtained and always are obtained only at the expense of the welfare and greatness of other nations and states.

It would seem to be obvious that patriotism as a sentiment is bad and harmful; as a doctrine it is stupid, since it is clear that if every nation and state shall consider itself the best of nations and states, all of them will find themselves in a gross and harmful error.

2

One would think that the harmfulness and irrationality of patriotism ought to be obvious to men. But, strange to say, enlightened, learned men not only fail to see this, but also with the greatest persistency and fervour, though without any rational foundations, refute every indication of the harmfulness and irrationality of patriotism, and continue to laud is beneficence and exalted condition.

What does that mean?

Only one explanation of this remarkable phenomenon presents itself to me. The whole history of humanity, from the most remote times to the present, may be viewed as the motion of the consciousness of separate individuals and of homogeneous aggregates of them from lower to higher ideas.

The whole path traversed both by each individual person and the homogeneous groups of men may be considered as a consecutive series of steps, from the lowest, which is on a level with the animal life, to the highest, which at a given historical moment may be reached by the consciousness of man.

Every man, like the separate homogeneous groups,—the nations, the states,—has always walked, as it were, over the steps of ideas. Some parts of humanity march on, others fall far behind, and others again, the majority, move in the middle. But all of them, no matter on what step they may be standing, having behind them the obsolete recollections of the past, and ahead of them the ideals of the future, are always in a process of struggling between the obsolete ideas of the past and the ideas of the future, which are just entering into life. What generally takes place is this, that when an idea, which in the past was useful and even indispensable, becomes superfluous, this idea, after a more or less prolonged struggle, gives way to a new idea, which heretofore was an ideal, but now becomes the idea of the present.

But it also happens that the obsolete idea, which in the consciousness of men has already given way to the higher idea, is such that the maintenance of this obsolete idea is advantageous for some people, who have the greatest influence in society. And then it happens that this obsolete idea, in spite of its sharp contradiction to the whole structure of life, which is changed in the other relations, continues to influence men and to guide them in their acts. Such a retardation of an obsolete idea has always taken place in the sphere of religion. The reason of it is this, that the priests, whose advantageous position is connected with the obsolete religious idea, making use of their power, intentionally retain the obsolete idea in the minds of men.

The same takes place, and for the same reason, in the political sphere, in relation to the idea of patriotism, on which every state structure is based. Men who profit by it artificially maintain this idea, which no longer has any sense or use. They are able to do so, since they are in possession of the most powerful means for influencing men.

In this do I find an explanation of the strange contradiction between the obsolete idea of patriotism and the whole contrary train of ideas, which in our time have already passed into the consciousness of the Christian world.

3

Patriotism, as a sentiment of exclusive love for one's nation and as a doctrine about the virtuous sacrifice of one's peace, property, and even life for the defense of the weak against the murderousness and violence of their enemies, was the highest idea of a time when every nation considered it possible and just, for the sake of its own good and greatness, to subject the men of another nation to murder and pillage; but as far back as two thousand years ago, the highest representatives of the wisdom of humanity began to recognize the higher idea of the brotherhood of men, and this idea, entering the consciousness more and more, has in our time received the most varied realization. Thanks to the greater ease of intercommunication, the unification of industry, commerce, the arts and the sciences, the men of our time are so united among themselves that the danger of conquests, slaughter, and violence on the part of neighbouring nations has entirely disappeared, and all the nations (the nations, not the governments) live among themselves in peaceful, mutually advantageous, amicable, industrial, commercial, mental relations, which they have no reason and no need to violate. And so it would seem that the obsolete feeling of patriotism ought to be destroyed more and more and to vanish completely, as superfluous and incompatible with the vitalized consciousness of the brotherhood of the men of the various nationalities. However, the reverse takes place: this harmful and obsolete sentiment not only continues to exist, but is even fanned more and more.

The nations without any rational foundation, contrary to their consciousness and their advantages, not only sympathize with the governments in their attacks upon other nations, in their seizures of the possessions of others, and in the use of violence in defending what has already been seized,— but themselves demand these attacks, seizures, and defenses, and rejoice in them and are proud of them. The minor oppressed nationalities, which have fallen into the power of the larger states,—the Poles, the Irish, the Bohemians, the Finns,

the Armenians,—reacting against the patriotism of the conquerors, which is crushing them, have to such an extent become infected by the oppressing nations with the obsolete,
useless, senseless, and harmful sentiment of patriotism, that
their whole activity is centred upon it, and they themselves,
suffering from the patriotism of the powerful nations, are
prepared out of the same patriotism to do to the other nations
the same that the nations which have conquered them have
been doing to them.

This is due to the fact that the ruling classes (meaning
by this not merely the governments with their officials, but
also all the classes which enjoy an exclusive, advantageous
position,—the capitalists, journalists, the majority of artists
and scholars) are able to retain their exclusive and advantageous position, as compared with the popular masses, only
thanks to the political structure which is supported by means
of patriotism. By having in their hands all the most powerful means for influencing the masses, they always unswervingly maintain the patriotic feelings in themselves and in
others, the more so, since these sentiments, which support the
power of the state, are more than any other rewarded by that
power.

Every official succeeds in his service in proportion to his patriotism; even so a military man can advance in his career
only in a war, which is provoked by patriotism.

Patriotism and its consequences, the wars, give a good
income to the newspaper men and advantages to the majority
of merchants. Every author, teacher, professor, will make his
position the more secure, the more he preaches patriotism.
Every emperor and king gains glory in proportion to his de-
votion to patriotism.

The army, the money, the school, the religion, the press,
is in the hands of the ruling classes. In the schools they fan
patriotism in the children by means of history, by describing
their nation as the best of all the nations and always in the
right; in the adults the same sentiment is roused by means of
spectacles, celebrations, monuments, and a patriotic, lying

press; but patriotism is chiefly roused in them by this, that, committing all kinds of unjust acts and cruelties against other nations, they provoke in these nations a hatred for their own nation, and then use this hatred for provoking such a hatred in their own nation.

The fanning of this terrible sentiment of patriotism has proceeded in the European nations in a rapidly increasing progression, and in our time has reached a stage beyond which it cannot go.

4

Within the memory of all, not merely old men of our time, there took place an event which in the most obvious manner showed the striking stupefaction to which the men of the Christian world were brought by means of patriotism.

The German ruling classes fanned the patriotism of their popular masses to such an extent that in the second half of the century a law was proposed to the people, according to which all men without exception were to become soldiers; all sons, husbands, fathers, were to study murder and to become submissive slaves of the first highest rank, and to be prepared for the murder of those whom they would be ordered to kill, —the men of the oppressed nationalities and their own labourers who should defend their rights,—their fathers and brothers, as the most impudent of all rulers, William II., publicly announced.

This terrible measure, which in the rudest way offends all the best sentiments of men, has, under the influence of patriotism, been accepted without a murmur by the nation of Germany.

The consequence of this was the victory over the French. This victory still more fanned the patriotism of Germany, and later of France, Russia, and other powers, and all the people of the Continental powers without a murmur submitted to the introduction of a universal military service, that is, to slavery, which for the degree of degradation and loss of will cannot be compared with any of the ancient conditions of slavery. After that, the slavish submission of the masses in the name of patriotism, and the impudence, cruelty, and madness of the governments knew no bounds. There began a mad race, provoked partly by lust, partly by vanity, and partly by greed, for the seizure of foreign lands in Asia, Africa, and America, and a greater and ever greater mistrust and fury of the governments against one another.

The destruction of nations on seized lands was taken as something self-evident. The only question was as to who was going to be the first to seize the land and to destroy its inhabitants. All the rulers have not only in the most obvious manner violated the most primitive demands of justice against the vanquished nations and against one another, but have also practiced all kinds of deceptions, rascalities, briberies, forgeries, espionage, pillage, and murder, and the nations have not only failed to sympathize with all that, but have even rejoiced, because their states, and not foreign states, have been committing these evil deeds. The mutual enmity of the nations and states has of late reached such wonderful dimensions that, although there is no reason why one state should attack other states, all know that all the states are all the time standing opposite one another extending their claws and showing their teeth, and just waiting for some one to fall into misfortune and grow feeble, in order to be able with the least danger to attack him and tear him to pieces.

All the nations of the so-called Christian world have been brought by patriotism to such a degree of bestialization that not only the men who are put to the necessity of killing or being killed, wish for and rejoice at murder, but also the men who calmly live in their houses in Europe, who are not threatened by any one, thanks to the rapid and easy means of communication and to the press,—all men in Europe and in America,—during any war are in the position of spectators in a Roman circus, and just like them rejoice at the slaughter, and just as bloodthirstily cry, *"Pollice verso!"*

Not only the adults, but also the children, the pure, wise children, according to the nationality to which they belong, rejoice, when they hear that not seven hundred, but one thousand Englishmen or Boers were killed and torn to pieces by lyddite shells. And the parents, I know such, encourage their children in such bestiality.

But more than that. Every increase of the army of one state (and every state, being on account of patriotism in danger, wishes to increase it) compels the neighbouring state to increase its army also for the sake of patriotism, which again calls forth a new increase of the first.

The same is true of the fortresses and fleets: one state builds ten ironclads, so the neighbouring ones build eleven; then the first builds twelve, and so on in an endless progression.

"I'll pinch you."—"And I'll strike you with my fist."—"I'll whip you."—"And I'll club you."—"I'll shoot you." Thus quarrel and fight only bad children, drunken men, or animals, and yet it is this that is taking place in the midst of the highest representatives of the most enlightened states, the same that are guiding the education and morality of their subjects.

5

The state of affairs is getting worse and worse, and there is no possibility whatever of arresting this degeneration, which is leading to certain ruin. The only way out from this situation, as credulous people thought, is now closed by the events of recent times: I am speaking of The Hague conference, and the war between England and the Transvaal, which followed immediately after.

If people who think little or only superficially were able to console themselves with the idea that international tribunals can remove the calamities of war and the evergrowing armaments, The Hague conference, with the war which followed upon its heels, in the most obvious manner showed the impossibility of solving the question in this manner. After The Hague conference it became obvious that so long as there shall exist governments with armies, the cessation of armaments and wars is impossible. For an agreement to be possible, it is necessary for the persons agreeing to believe one another. But for the powers to believe one another, they must lay down their arms, as do bearers of truce, when they come together for a consultation.

But so long as governments do not believe one another, not only do not destroy or diminish, but, on the contrary, keep increasing their armies, in conformity with the increase among their neighbours, and unswervingly through spies watch every movement of the armies, knowing that every power will attack the neighbouring one as soon as it shall have a chance to do so, no agreement is possible, and every conference is either a piece of stupidity, or a plaything, or a deception, or a piece of impudence, or all these things taken together.

It behooved the Russian government, more than any other, to become the *enfant terrible* of this conference. The Russian government is so spoiled by the fact that at home no one retorts to all those obviously lying manifestoes and rescripts, that, having without the least scruples ruined its own nation by means of armaments, having choked Poland, robbed Turkestan and China, and strangled Finland with particular fury, it proposed to the governments to disarm themselves, with the full conviction that it would be believed.

But, no matter how strange, how unexpected, and how indecent this proposition was, especially at a time when orders had been given to increase the armies, the words, enunciated in the hearing of all, were such that the governments of the other powers could not before their nations decline to participate in the comical, patently deceptive consultations, and the delegates came together, knowing in advance that nothing could come of it, and in the course of several months, during which they received good salaries, though they laughed in their sleeves, all of them good-naturedly pretended that they were busy establishing peace among the nations.

The Hague conference, which ended in terrible bloodshed, —the Transvaal war,—which no one has tried to stop, was none the less useful, though in a different way from what was expected from it: it was useful in that it showed in the most obvious manner that the evil from which the nations suffer cannot be mended by the governments, and that the governments, even if they wished to do so, are unable to abolish either armaments or wars. In order to be able to exist, the governments must defend their nations against attacks from other nations, but no nation wants to attack another, or ever does attack another, and so the governments not only do not wish for peace, but even make efforts to rouse the hatred of the other nations toward their own. Having roused the hatred of the other nations toward their own, and patriotism in their own nations, the governments assure their people that they are in danger and must defend themselves.

Having the power in their hands, the governments are able to irritate the other nations and to evoke patriotism in their own, and they use every effort to do both, nor can they themselves help doing so, because upon this is their existence based.

If the governments were needed before to defend their people against attacks from other nations, now, on the contrary, the governments artificially violate the peace which exists among the nations, and provoke hostilities among them.

When it is necessary to plough, in order to be able to sow, ploughing was a sensible thing; but it is evident that it is senseless and harmful to plough, after the crops have grown up. And yet it is precisely this that the governments make their nations do,—destroy that union which exists and would not be impaired by anything, if there were no governments.

6

Indeed, what are in our time those governments, without which it seems impossible for men to be able to exist?

If there was a time when the governments were a necessary and lesser evil than the one which resulted from defenselessness in relation to organized neighbours, the governments have now become an unnecessary and much greater evil than all that with which they frighten their nations.

The governments, not only the military ones, but the governments in general, could be, I do not say useful, but harmless, only in case they consisted of infallible, holy people, as is assumed to be the case in China. But the governments, by dint of their very activity, which consists in the practice of violence, are always composed of elements which are the very opposite of holy,—of the most impudent, coarse, and corrupted men.

For this reason every government, and especially every government to which the military power is delegated, is a most dangerous institution in the world.

The government, in its broadest sense, with the inclusion of capitalists and the press, is nothing but an organization such that the great majority of men are in the power of the minority, which stands above them; but this minority submits itself to the power of a still more restricted minority, and this again to a still more restricted minority, and so forth, reaching at last one man or a few men, who by means of military violence gain the power over all the rest. Thus this whole structure is like a cone, all the parts of which are in the full power of the few persons, or the person, at the apex of the cone.

But the apex of this cone is seized by those men, or by that man, who is more cunning, more bold, and more unscrupulous than the rest, or an accidental heir of those who were bolder and more unscrupulous.

To-day it is Borís Godunóv, to-morrow—Grigóri Otrépev; to-day—the harlot Catherine, who with her paramours strangled her husband, to-morrow—Pugachév, the day after—mad Paul, Nicholas, Alexander III.

To-day—Napoleon, to-morrow—Bourbon or Orleans, Boulanger, or a company of Panamaists; to-day—Gladstone, to-morrow—Salisbury, Chamberlain, Rhodes.

And it is such governments that are invested with full power, not only over property and life, but also over the spiritual and moral development, over the education, the religious guidance of all men.

Men produce this terrible machine of power, letting any one who pleases seize this power (and all the chances are that it will be seized by the one who is morally worst), and slavishly submit to it, and marvel that they are faring badly. They are afraid of mines, of anarchists, and are not afraid of that terrible structure, which threatens them any minute with the greatest calamities.

Men found that, to defend themselves against enemies, it is useful for them to tie themselves together, as the Circassians do, when defending themselves. But there is no danger, and men still continue to tie themselves.

They carefully tie themselves in such a way that one man is enabled to do with them what he pleases; then they allow the end of the rope which binds them to dangle about, leaving it to the first rascal or fool to take it up and do with them what he wants.

Is it not precisely what the nations are doing, when they submit, and establish and support a government which is organized with military power?

7

To free people from those terrible calamities of armaments and wars, which they suffer now, and which keep growing greater and greater, we do not need congresses, nor conferences, nor treaties and tribunals, but the abolition of that implement of violence which is called the governments, and from which originate all the greatest calamities of men.

To abolish the governments only one thing is needed: it is necessary that men should understand that the sentiment of patriotism, which alone maintains this implement of violence, is a coarse, harmful, disgraceful, and bad, and above all, immoral sentiment. It is coarse, because it is characteristic of only such men as stand on the lowest stage of morality and who expect from other nations the same acts of violence that they want to practice themselves; it is harmful, because it violates the advantageous and joyous peaceful relations with other nations, and, above all, produces that organization of the governments, in which the worst man can acquire and always acquires the power; it is disgraceful, because it transforms the man not only into a slave, but also into a fighting cock, bull, gladiator, who ruins his forces and his life, not for his own purposes, but for those of his government; it is immoral, because, instead of recognizing himself as the son of God, as Christianity teaches us, or at least as a free man, who is guided by his reason,—every man, under the influence of patriotism, recognizes himself as the son of his country, the slave of his government, and commits acts which are contrary to his reason and to his conscience.

Men need but understand this, and the terrible concatenation of men, called the government, will fall of its own accord, without any struggle, and with it will fall that terrible, useless evil which is caused by it to the nations.

Men are beginning to see this. This is, for example, what a citizen of the United States writes:

"The one thing which we all, farmers, mechanics, merchants, manufacturers, teachers, ask is the right to attend to our own business. We have our homes, love our friends, are devoted to our families, and do not interfere in the affairs of our neighbours,—we have our work, and we want to work.

"Leave us alone!

"But the politicians will not leave us alone. They impose taxes upon us, eat up our sustenance, keep a census of us, call our youths to their wars.

"Whole myriads of those who live at the expense of the government are maintained by them, in order to impose taxes upon us; but to tax us successfully, permanent armies are maintained. The argument that the army is needed for the defense of the country is an obvious deception. The French government frightens the people by saying that the Germans are about to attack them; the Russians are afraid of the English; the English are afraid of everybody else; and now

we are told in America that it is necessary to increase the
fleet and to add to the army, because Europe may at any
moment unite against us. That is a deception and a lie. The
common people in France, in Germany, in England, and in
America are against war. All we wish is to be left alone. The
men who have wives, parents, children, homes, have no desire
to go away to fight with anybody. We are peaceable and
fear war,—we hate it.

"All we want is not to do to others what we do not want
others to do to us.

"War is a direct consequence of the existence of armed
men. A country which maintains a large permanent army
will fight sooner or later. A man who is proud of his strength
in a wrestling match will some day meet a man who considers
himself a champion wrestler, and they will fight. Germany
and France are only waiting for a chance to try their strength.
They have fought several times and will fight again. Not
that the masses wish for war, but that the upper classes fan
in them their mutual hatred and compel people to think that
they must fight in order to defend themselves.

"Men who would like to follow Christ's teaching are taxed,
insulted, deceived, and drawn into the army.

"Christ taught meekness, humility, forgiveness of sins, and
that it is bad to kill. Scripture teaches people not to swear,
but the 'upper classes' compel us to swear on the Scripture,
in which they do not believe.

"How can we be freed from these spendthrifts, who do
not work, but who are dressed in fine cloth with brass but-
tons and costly ornaments, who are supported by our labours,
for whom we till the soil?

"Shall we fight with them?

"But we do not recognize bloodshed, and, besides, they
have the arms and the money, and they can stand it longer
than we.

"But who composes the army that will fight us?

"This army is formed by us, our deceived neighbours and
brothers, who have been made to believe that they are serv-

ing God, when they defend their country from the enemy. In reality our country has no enemies except the upper classes, who have taken upon themselves to guard our interests, if only we shall consent to pay the imposts. They consume our sustenance and rouse our true brothers against us, in order to enslave and degrade us.

"You cannot send a telegram to your wife, or your friend, or your commission dealer, unless you first pay a revenue, which is being collected for the maintenance of armed men, who may be used for the purpose of killing you, and who will unquestionably put you in jail, if you do not pay it.

"The only means consists in impressing people with the idea that it is bad to kill, in teaching them that the whole law and the prophets demand that we should not do to others what we do not wish that others should do to us. Silently disregard these upper classes, and refuse to bow before their martial idol. Stop supporting preachers who preach war and put forward patriotism as something important.

"Let them go and work, as we do.

"We believe in Christ, but they do not. Christ said what he thought; they say what they think will please the men in power,—'the upper class.'

"We will not enter military service. We will not shoot at their command. We will not arm ourselves with bayonets against the good and meek masses. We will not at the suggestion of Cecil Rhodes shoot at shepherds and agriculturists, who are defending their hearths.

"Your deceptive cry 'Wolf, wolf!' does not frighten us. We pay our imposts only because we are compelled to do so. We will pay them only so long as we are compelled to do so. We will not pay any church tribute to the hypocrites, nor our tithes for your hypocritical philanthropy, and we will on every occasion express our opinion.

"We will educate the men.

"And all the time our silent influence will grow; even the soldiers who have been drafted into the army will waver before fighting. We will preach the idea that the Christian life in peace and good-will is better than a life of struggle, bloodshed, and war.

"Peace on earth will come only when men shall separate themselves from the armies and will wish to do to others what they wish that others should do to them."

Thus writes a citizen of the United States of North America, and on all sides and in all forms similar voices are heard.

Here is what a German soldier writes:

"I have taken part in two expeditions of the Prussian Guard (1866, 1870), and I hate war from the depth of my heart, since it has made me inexpressibly unhappy. We, the wounded warriors, receive for the most part such miserable rewards, that we really have to be ashamed of having ever been patriots. I, for example, receive daily eighty pfennigs for my disabled arm, which was shot through at the storming of Saint Privas, on August 18, 1870. Many a hunting dog needs more for its maintenance. I have suffered for years from my disabled right arm. As early as 1866 I took part in the war against the Austrians, fighting at Trautenau and Königgrätz, and I have seen a lot of horrors. In 1870 I, being in the reserve, was again called out, and, as I have already said, I was wounded at the storming of Saint Privas: my right arm was twice shot down its whole length. I lost a good place (I was then a beer brewer), and after that I could not get it back. Since then I have never been able to get on my legs again. The intoxication has passed away, and the invalid warrior has nothing to live on but a beggar's pittance and alms. . . .

"In a world in which men run about like trained animals and are not capable of any other idea than that of outwitting one another for the sake of mammon, I may be considered an odd person, but I none the less feel in myself the divine idea of peace, which is so beautifully expressed in the Sermon on the Mount. According to my innermost conviction war is nothing but commerce on a large scale,—a commerce of the ambitious and mighty in the happiness of the nations.

"What horrors one passes through in connection with it!

I shall never forget them, those pitiful groans, which penetrate me to the marrow of my bones.

"Men who have never done any evil to one another slay one another like wild animals, and petty souls of slaves draw the good God into it as an accomplice in these acts.

"My neighbour in the ranks had his jaws shattered by a bullet. The unfortunate man was insane from pain. He ran about like a madman, and in the burning summer heat was unable to find some water with which to cool his terrible wound. Our commander, Crown Prince Frederick (later the noble Emperor Frederick) at that time wrote in his diary, 'War is an irony on the Gospel.' . . ."

Men are beginning to understand the deception of patriotism, in which all the governments are trying so zealously to maintain them.

8

"But what will happen when there shall be no more governments?" people generally ask.

There will be nothing; what will happen will be this, that which long ago ceased to be useful and now is superfluous and bad will be destroyed; what will be destroyed is the organ which, having become useless, has grown to be harmful.

"But if there shall be no governments, people will violate and kill one another," people generally say.

Why? Why will the abolition of an organization, which arose as the result of violence and which has been transmitted from generation to generation for the purpose of exerting violence,—why will the abolition of such an obsolete organization cause people to violate and kill one another? It would seem, on the contrary, that the destruction of the organ of violence would have the effect that people would stop practicing violence and killing one another.

There now are people who are specially educated and prepared for killing and violating men,—people to whom the right to commit acts of violence is delegated, and who make use of

an organization which is established for the purpose; and such
violence and murder is considered to be a good and virtuous
act. Then people will not be educated for the purpose, no
one will have the right to do violence to others, there will be
no organization of violence, and as is not the case with the
men of our time, violence and murder will always and by all
men be considered to be a bad thing.

If after the destruction of the governments acts of violence
shall be committed, it is evident that they will be less than
those at the present time, when there exist organizations
specially established for the production of violence, and when
there are conditions when violence and murder are considered
good and useful.

The abolition of the governments will only destroy the tra-
ditional, useless organization of violence and its justification.

"There will be no laws, no property, no courts, no police,
no popular education," people generally say, intentionally con-
fusing the violence of the power with the different activities
of society.

The abolition of the organization of governments, which
are established for the purpose of exerting violence against
people, does not bring with it the destruction of what is
rational and good, and so what is non-violating in the laws,
the courts, the property, the police defense, the financial institutions, the popular education. On the contrary, the absence of the rude power of the governments, whose only purpose is to support themselves, will contribute to a more rational and just public organization, which is in no need of
violence. Courts, public affairs, and popular education, all
that will exist to the extent to which the nations shall need
them, and in a form which will not contain any evil that is
connected with the present governmental organization; only
that will be destroyed which was bad and interfered with the
free manifestation of the will of the nations.

But even if we admit that with the absence of the governments there will occur disturbances and inner conflicts, the
state of affairs would even in that case be better than what it

is now. The present condition of the nations is such that it is hard to imagine it worse. The masses are all ruined, and the ruin must inevitably keep growing greater. All the men are turned into military slaves and must at any moment await the command to go out and kill and be killed. For what else shall they wait? That the ruined nations shall starve to death? That, indeed, is now taking place in Russia, Italy, and India. Or that not only the men, but also the women shall be drafted into the army? In the Transvaal they are beginning to do so.

Thus, even if the absence of government should actually mean anarchy in the negative, disorderly sense of the word (which it does not at all mean), no disorders of anarchy could be worse than the condition to which the governments have already brought their nations and toward which they are leading them.

And so the liberation from patriotism and the destruction of the despotism of the governments which is based upon it cannot help but be useful to people.

9

Bethink yourselves, people, and, for the sake of your bodily and spiritual good, and for the same good of your brothers and sisters, stop, think, reflect on what you are doing!

Bethink yourselves and understand that not the Boers, English, French, Germans, Bohemians, Finns, Russians are your enemies, but that the only enemies are you yourselves, who with your patriotism support the governments, which oppress you and cause your misfortunes.

They undertook to defend you against dangers, and have carried this condition of defense to such an extent that you have all become soldiers and slaves, that you are all ruined, that you are being ruined more and more, and may and must expect at any moment the breaking of the strained string and the terrible slaughter of you and your children.

No matter how great the slaughter may be and how it

may end, the condition will remain the same. Even so and with still greater tension will the governments arm and destroy and corrupt you and your children, and no one will help you to stop it all, if you are not going to help yourselves.

There is but one help, and that is to destroy that terrible concatenation of the cone of violence, with which those who succeed in getting to the apex of the cone dominate the whole nation, and dominate the more surely, the more cruel and inhuman they are, as we know from the case of Napoleon, Nicholas I., Bismarck, Chamberlain, Rhodes, and our dictators who rule the nation in the name of the Tsar.

There is but one means for destroying this concatenation, and that is, to awaken from the hypnosis of patriotism.

You must understand that all the evil from which you suffer you are causing yourselves, in that you submit to those suggestions by means of which you are deceived by the emperors, kings, members of parliaments, rulers, military men, capitalists, clergy, authors, artists,—by all those who need this deception of patriotism in order to be able to live by your labours.

Whoever you may be,—a Frenchman, Russian, Pole, Englishman, Irishman, German, Bohemian,—you must understand that all our real human interests, whatever they be,—agricultural, industrial, commercial, artistic, or scientific,—all these interests, like all the pleasures and joys, in no way oppose the interests of the other nations and states, and that you are, by means of a mutual interaction, exchange of services, the joy of a broad brotherly communion, of an exchange not only of wares, but also of sentiments, united with the men of the other nations.

You must understand that the questions as to who succeeds in seizing Wei-hai-wei, Port Arthur, or Cuba—whether it is your government or another—are by no means a matter of indifference to you, but that every seizure made by your government is detrimental to you, because it inevitably brings with it all kinds of influences, which your government will exert against you, in order to compel you to take part in robberies and acts of violence, which are necessary for the seizures and for the retention of what has been seized. You must understand that your life can in no way be improved by this, that Alsace will be German or French, and that Ireland and Poland are free or enslaved: no matter whose they may be, you can live wherever you please; even if you were an Alsatian, an Irishman, or a Pole,—you must understand that every fanning of patriotism will only make your position worse, because the enslavement of your nation has resulted only from the struggle of patriotisms, and that every manifestation of patriotism in one nation increases the reaction against it in another. You must understand that you can save yourselves from all your calamities only when you free yourselves from the obsolete idea of patriotism and from the obedience to the governments which is based upon it, and when you shall boldly enter into the sphere of that higher idea of the brotherly union of the nations, which has long ago entered into life and is calling you to itself from all sides.

Let men understand that they are not the sons of any countries or governments, but the sons of God, and that, therefore, they cannot be slaves, nor enemies of other men, and all those senseless, now quite useless, pernicious institutions, bequeathed by antiquity, which are called governments, and all those sufferings, acts of violence, degradations, crimes, which they bring with them, will disappear of their own accord.

Pirógovo, May 10, 1900.

SHAME!

(1895)

In the twenties of the nineteenth century the officers of the Seménovski Regiment, the flower of the youths of that day, for the most part Masons and subsequently Decembrists, decided not to use any corporal punishment in their regiment, and, in spite of the strict demands of military service at that time, the regiment continued to be a model one, even without the application of corporal punishment.

One of the commanders of a company of the Seménovski Regiment, upon meeting one day Sergyéy Ivánovich Muravév, one of the best men of that, and indeed of any, time, told him about one of his soldiers, a thief and drunkard, saying that such a soldier could not be brought to his senses in any other way than by means of the rod. Sergyéy Muravév did not agree with him and offered to take the soldier in his company.

The transfer was made, and the soldier in the very first days stole a pair of boots from his comrade, and with the proceeds from the sale of them got drunk, and acted riotously. Sergyéy Ivánovich called together the company and, calling the soldier to the front, said to him: "You know that in my company soldiers are not beaten or flogged, and I will not have you punished. For the boots which you stole I will pay with my own money, and I beg of you, not for my sake, but for your own sake, to reflect upon your life and to change it." And, having given the soldier friendly instructions, Sergyéy Ivánovich dismissed him.

The soldier again got drunk and had a fight. And again he was not punished, but only admonished: "You will only

97

harm yourself the more; but if you mend your ways, you will be the better off for it. For this reason I ask you not to do such things."

The soldier was so surprised at this new way of being treated that he changed completely and became a model soldier.

The narrator of this story, Sergyéy Ivánovich's brother, Matvyéy Ivánovich, who, like his brother and all the best men of the time, considered corporal punishment to be a disgraceful remainder of barbarism, disgraceful not so much for the man punished, as for the men punishing, never could keep back tears of emotion and transport, when he spoke of it, and it was equally impossible to restrain tears, when listening to him.

Thus corporal punishment was viewed by cultured Russians seventy-five years ago. Now seventy-five years have passed, and in our time the grandchildren of these men preside in the capacity of County Council chiefs in courts and calmly discuss the question whether rods are to be administered or not, and how many rods are to be given to such and such an adult, a father of a family, often a grandfather.

But the leaders among these grandchildren sitting in committees and County Council assemblies hand in memorandums, addresses, and petitions, asking, in the name of hygienic and pedagogical purposes, that not all the peasants, but only those who have not finished a course in a popular school, be subject to flogging.

An enormous change has taken place in the midst of the so-called higher cultured class. The men of the twenties, considering corporal punishment to be a disgraceful act for themselves, found a way for abolishing it in the army, where it was thought to be indispensable; but the men of our time calmly apply it, not to the soldiers, but to all men of one of the classes of the Russian people, and cautiously, diplomatically, in committees and assemblies, with every imaginable excuse and circumlocution, address and petition the government as to this, that the punishment with rods does not com-

ply with the demands of hygiene and so must be limited, or
that it would be desirable to flog only such peasants as have
not finished a course in the rudiments, or that the peasants
who are included in the manifesto on the occasion of the
emperor's marriage may be exempted from corporal punishment.

Obviously a terrible change has taken place in the midst
of the so-called higher Russian society, and, what is most
remarkable, this change has taken place at a time when in the
very class, which, it is assumed necessary to make submit to
the disgusting, coarse, and stupid torture of flogging, there
has in the last seventy-five years, especially in the last thirty-
five years, since the liberation, taken place just such a vast
change, only in the opposite direction.

While the higher, ruling classes have coarsened and morally
fallen to such an extent that they have legalized flogging and
calmly discuss the same, there has in the peasant class taken
place such an uplifting of the mental and moral level that the
application of corporal punishment to this class appears to
the men of this class not only as a physical, but also as a moral
torture.

I have heard and read of cases of suicide among peasants
condemned to rods, and I cannot refuse to believe this, because I saw myself an ordinary young peasant, at the mere
mention in the township court of the possibility of admin-
istering corporal punishment to him, grow as pale as a sheet
and lose his voice; I saw also another peasant, of about forty
years of age, who was condemned to corporal punishment,
burst out weeping, when, in reply to my question whether
the decree of the court was carried out, he had to answer that
it was.

I know also of a case where an acquaintance of mine, a
respectable, middle-aged peasant, who was condemned to
be flogged for having, as usual, called the stárosta names,
without paying attention to the fact that the stárosta wore
the insignia, was taken to the township office, and from there
to the shed where the punishment is administered.   The

watchman came with the rods, and the peasant was told to take off his clothes.

"Parmén Ermílych, I have a married son," said the peasant, turning to the township elder, and shaking with his whole body. "Can't this be omitted? It is a sin."

"The government, Petróvich,—I should gladly,—what is to be done?" replied the embarrassed elder.

Petróvich took off his clothes and lay down.

"Christ has suffered and told us to suffer," he said.

As the scribe who was present told me, everybody's arms trembled, and nobody dared to look into his neighbour's eyes, feeling that they were doing something terrible. And these people it is assumed indispensable and apparently useful for some one to flog like beasts,—indeed, even animals are not allowed to be tortured.

For the good of our Christian and enlightened state it is indispensable to subject to a most insipid, indecent, and offensive punishment, not all the members of this Christian enlightened state, but only one of its classes, the most industrious, useful, moral, and numerous.

The highest authorities of an enormous Christian state have not been able nineteen centuries after Christ to invent something more useful, clever, and moral for the counteraction of violation of laws than that the people who have violated the laws, grown men, and sometimes old men, be undressed, thrown on the floor, and beaten with rods on their backsides.*

And the men of our time, who consider themselves to be leaders, the grandsons of the men who seventy-five years ago destroyed capital punishment, now most humbly and quite seriously ask the minister or some one else not to subject to flogging the adult Russians so much, because the doctors find this unhealthy, not to subject to flogging those who have finished a course, and to free from flogging those who should

* Why this particular stupid, savage method of causing pain, and no other? Why not stick pins into the shoulder or some other part of the body, compress the hands or feet in a vise, or something like that?— *Author's Note.*

be flogged immediately after the emperor's marriage. But the wise government keeps profound silence in response to such frivolous requests or even prohibits them.

But is it possible to ask about these things? Can there be a question about them? There are certain acts, whether they be committed by private individuals, or by governments, which cannot be discussed coolly, condemning the commission of these acts only under certain conditions. And the flogging of adults from one of the classes of the Russian nation in our time, amidst our meek and enlightened Christian people, belongs to this class of acts. It is not right for the abatement of the transgression of all divine and human laws diplomatically to approach the government on the score of hygiene, school education, or the manifesto. Such things must either not be mentioned at all, or must be talked about as to their essence and always with contempt and horror. To ask that only such peasants as have finished the rudiments be not switched over their bare hips, is the same as if, where the punishment of an adulterous woman was that she be taken naked through the city, one should ask that the punishment be applied only to those women who do not know how to knit stockings, or something like that.

About such things people cannot "ask most humbly" and "prostrate themselves before one's feet," and so forth; such things can and must be only arraigned. Such things must be arraigned, because these things, when the aspect of legality is given to them, only disgrace us all, who live in the state where such acts are committed. Indeed, if the flogging of the peasants is a law, this law is made for me as much as for anybody, to secure my peace and well-being, but this cannot be admitted.

I do not want and am not able to recognize a law which violates all the divine and human laws, and I cannot imagine myself of one accord with those who write and confirm such crimes under the form of law.

If we have to speak at all of this monstrousness, we can say only this, that there can be no such law, that no ukases,

Mirrors of Law, signatures, or command of his Majesty can make a law of a crime, and that, on the contrary, the vesting of such a crime (as this, that the adults of but one, the best class, may at the will of another, a worse class,—that of the gentry and officials,—be subjected to an indecent, savage, disgusting punishment) with the form of law proves better than anything else that where such an imaginary legalization of a crime is possible no laws exist, but only savage arbitrariness of rude power.

If we must speak at all of the corporal punishment which is administered to but one, the peasant class, we must not defend the rights of the County Council assembly or complain to the minister of the governor who protested against the solicitations about stopping the flogging of those who know how to read, or complain to the senate of the minister, or complain still higher up of the senate, as was proposed by the Tambóv County Council, but must never stop crying and shouting that the application of this savage punishment, which is no longer used in the case of children, to one, the best class of Russians, is a disgrace for all those who take part in it directly or indirectly.

Petróvich, who lay down to receive the rods, making the sign of the cross and saying, "Christ suffered and told us to suffer," forgave his tormentors and after the rods remained what he had been. The torture accomplished upon him could have had but one result, that of making him despise the power which can prescribe such punishments. But on many young men not only the punishment itself, but frequently the mere acknowledgment that it is possible, has the effect of lowering their moral sense and provoking either desperation or brutality. But this is not yet the chief harm of this monstrousness. The chief harm consists in the mental condition of those men who establish, permit, and prescribe this illegality, those men who use it as a threat, and all those who live in the conviction that such a violation of all justice and humanity is necessary for a good, regular life. What a terrible maiming there must be in the brains and hearts of such men, frequently young men, who, as I myself have heard, assert with an aspect of profound wisdom that it is impossible not to flog the peasant, and that it is better for the peasant that he should be flogged.

It is these people who are to be pitied most for the bestiality into which they have fallen and in which they abide.

Therefore the liberation of the Russian people from the corrupting influence of the legalized crime is in every way an affair of vast importance. This liberation will not take place when those who have finished a course, or any other peasants, or even all the peasants, with the exception of one single peasant, shall be exempted from corporal punishment, but only when the ruling classes will recognize their sin and shall meekly submit to it.

December 14, 1895.

CARTHAGO DELENDA EST

(1898)

La Vita Internazionale and L'Humanité Nouvelle sent me the following letter:

"MONSIEUR:—*Dans le but d'être utile au développement des idées humanitaires de la civilisation* La Vita Internazionale *(Milan), avec l'appui de* L'Humanité Nouvelle *(Paris et Bruxelles), a cru devoir s'intéresser au difficile problème qui dernièrement s'est montré dans toute sa gravité et son importance à cause de la délicate question pour laquelle la France et le monde entier se sont passionés si vivement: nous voulons parler du problème de la guerre et du militarisme. A cette fin, nous prions tous ceux qui en Europe dans la politique, les sciences, les arts, dans le mouvement ouvrier, parmi les militaires mêmes occupent la place la plus éminente, de contribuer à cette œuvre hautement civilisatrice en nous envoyant les réponses au questionnaire suivant:*

"*1. La guerre parmi les nations civilisées est-elle encore voulue par l'histoire, par le droit, par le progrès?*

"*2. Quels sont les effets intellectuels, moraux, physiques, économiques, politiques, du militarisme?*

"*3. Quelles sont les solutions qu'il convient de donner, dans l'intérêt de l'avenir de la civilisation mondiale, aux graves problèmes de la guerre et du militarisme?*

"*4. Quels sont les moyens conduisant le plus rapidement possible à ces solutions?*"

I cannot conceal that feeling of disgust, indignation, and even despair, which this letter provoked in me. People of our Christian world, enlightened, clever, good men, who profess the law of love and of brotherhood, who regard murder

as a terrible crime, who, with few exceptions, are unable to
kill an animal, all these people suddenly, under certain conditions, when these crimes are called war, not only recognize
destruction, pillage, and the murder of men to be right and
lawful, but themselves contribute to this pillage and these
murders, prepare themselves for them, take part in them, and
pride themselves on them. With this the same phenomenon is
always repeated, namely this, that a vast majority of men,
all the working people, those who do the pillaging and the
murdering and bear the whole weight of this business, do not
plan, or prepare, or wish these murders, and take part in them
against their will, only because they are placed in such a position and are so minded that it seems to them, to each of them
individually, that they will fare worse, if they refuse to take
part in these robberies and murders and in the preparations
for them; but it is only a very insignificant minority, which
lives in luxury and idleness upon the labours of the working
people, that plans and prepares those robberies and murders,
and compels the working people to commit them. This deception has been taking place for a long time, but of late
the impudence of the deceivers has reached the farthest limit:
a large portion of the products of labour are taken away from
the working people and are used for the preparations for
these robberies and murders. In all the constitutional governments of Europe, the labourers themselves, all without exception, are called upon to take part in these robberies and murders, the international relations are intentionally made more
and more complex, so as to lead up to war, peaceful countries
are robbed without any cause, every year people are robbed
and killed somewhere, and all men live in constant fear of
universal mutual pillage and murder. It would seem to be
obvious that if such a phenomenon takes place, it is due to
this, that the greater masses are deceived by the minority, to
which this deception is profitable, and that, therefore, the first
thing those who want to free people from the calamities of
these mutual robberies and murders ought to do is to lay open
the deception in which the masses are, to show the masses

how the deception is accomplished, how it is maintained, and how to be freed from it. But the enlightened men of Europe do nothing of the kind: instead of it they, under the pretext of coöperating with the establishment of peace, at first gather in one city of Europe, then in another, and seat themselves with most serious faces at tables and discuss in what way best to persuade the robbers, who live by their trade, to stop committing robberies and become peaceful citizens, and then they put profound questions: the first, as to whether history, right, progress demand war, as though the fictions which we invent can demand of us a departure from the fundamental moral law of our life; the second question,—as to what can be the consequences of war, as though there can be any doubt in this, that the consequences of war will always be universal calamity and universal corruption; and, finally, the third question, how to solve the problem of war, as though there existed a difficult problem about how to free deceived men from the deception which we see clearly.

This is terrible. We see, for example, that healthy, peaceable, often happy people from year to year frequent gambling-dens, such as Monte Carlo, and leave there, for the advantage of the keepers of these dens, their health, their peace, their honour, and frequently their lives. We are sorry for these men; we see clearly that the deception to which these people are subjected consists in those temptations by means of which the players are enticed, in the inequality of the chances, and in the infatuation of the players, who know that in general they will be losers, but none the less hope that they will at least once be more fortunate than others. All that is perfectly clear. And here, instead of freeing people from these calamities, instead of pointing out to them the temptations to which they are subjected, the certainty of their losses, the immorality of the play, which is based on the expectation of other people's misfortunes, we meet with distinguished men in sessions and discuss the questions as to how to arrange matters so that the keepers of the gambling establishments shall voluntarily close their institutions, we write books about this, and ask ourselves questions as to whether history, right, and progress do not demand the existence of gambling establishments, and what may be the consequences of roulette,—the economic, intellectual, moral consequences, etc.

If a man drinks, and I tell him that he can himself stop drinking and must do so, there is some hope that he will pay attention to me; but if I tell him that his drunkenness forms a complex and difficult problem, which we, the learned, will try to solve in our meetings, all the probabilities are that he, waiting for the solution of the problem, will continue to drink. The same is true of the false and intricate scientific, external means for the cessation of war, like the international tribunals, the court of arbitration, and other similar foolish things, when we with them keep in abeyance the simplest and most essential means for the cessation of war, which is only too obvious to anybody. For people who do not need war not to fight we need no international tribunals, no solution of questions, but only that the people who are subject to deception should awaken and free themselves from that spell under which they are. This means for the abolition of war consists in this, that the men who do not need war, who consider a participation in war to be a sin, should stop fighting. This means has been preached since the most remote times by Christian writers,— Tertullian, Origen, and by the Paulicians and their continuators, the Mennonites, the Quakers, the Herrnhuters; about this means wrote Dymond, Garrison, Ballou; it will soon be twenty years during which I have in every way elucidated the sin, harmfulness, and senselessness of military service. This means was applied long ago, and has been applied with particular frequency, both by separate individuals in Austria, Prussia, Switzerland, Holland, Sweden, Russia, and by whole societies, such as the Quakers, Mennonites, Nazarenes, and of late the Dukhobors, a whole fifteen thousand of whom have now for three years been struggling against the mighty Russian government, in spite of all the sufferings to which they are subjected, without acceding to its demands that they take part in the crimes of military service.

But the enlightened friends of peace not only do not propose this means,— they cannot even bear the mention of it; and when they hear of it, they make it appear that they do not notice it, or, if they notice it, they shrug their shoulders with a significant mein, expressing compassion for those uneducated and senseless people, who use such an inefficacious, stupid means, when they have such a good means, which consists in throwing salt on the tail of the bird which you want to catch, that is, in persuading the governments, which live only by violence and deception, to renounce this violence and deception.

They say that the misunderstandings that may arise between the governments will be decided by tribunals or by a court of arbitration. But the governments do not at all wish for the settling of these misunderstandings: on the contrary, the governments invent misunderstandings, if they do not exist, because only misunderstandings with other governments give them an opportunity of maintaining the army on which their power is based. Thus the enlightened friends of peace try to distract the attention of the suffering working people from the only means which frees them from the slavery, in which they are held from childhood by means of patriotism, and then by means of the venal priests of a corrupt Christianity, by binding men by an oath and, finally, threatening them with punishments.

In our time, when close peaceful relations have been established between the men of various nationalities and states, the deception of patriotism, which always demands the preference of one state or nationality to others, and which, therefore, always draws people into useless and ruinous wars, is too obvious for sensible people not to be freed from it; the deception of the obligatoriness of the religious oath, which is clearly forbidden in the Gospel professed by the governments, is, thank God, believed in less and less, so that it is only the fear of the punishment which is imposed on such refusals by the government, that for the majority of men serves as a barrier to refusing to take part in military service. But this fear, too, is only a consequence of the deception practised by the governments, and has no foundation but in hypnosis.

The governments may and must be afraid of those who refuse, and, in reality, are afraid of them, because every refusal undermines the prestige of the deception, in which the governments keep men, but those who refuse have no reason to fear the government which demands the crime. By refusing to do military service every man risks much less than in entering the army. The refusal to do military service, and the punishment,—imprisonment, exile,—are frequently only a profitable self-insurance from the dangers of military service. Upon entering military service a man risks taking part in war, for which he is being prepared, and of getting in the war into such a position that he will, under the most oppressive and agonizing of conditions, be certainly killed, like one condemned to death, or crippled, as, indeed, I saw at Sevastopol, where a regiment came to a bastion where two regiments had already been killed off, and remained there until it, too, was annihilated. A second, more advantageous eventuality is this, that the one who does military service will not be killed, but will only fall sick and die from the unhealthy conditions of military service. A third eventuality is this that, having been insulted, he will not hold out, will say something rude to his superior, will violate discipline, and will be subjected to a worse punishment than what he would suffer by refusing to do military service. The most advantageous eventuality is this, that, instead of imprisonment or deportation, to which he who refuses military service would be subjected, he will pass three or five years of his life in preparing himself to commit murder, in a corrupt circle and in a slavery similar to that in a prison, except for a degrading humility to corrupt men.

So much in the first place. In the second place, in refusing military service, every man, however improbable this may be, may none the less count on having to suffer no punishment, because his refusal will be that last arraignment of the government's deception, in consequence of which it will not be possible for any one to punish him, because no people will be found who are so stultified that they can coöperate in the punishment of the man who refuses to take part in their oppression. Thus the submission to the demands of military service is obviously only a submission to the hypnosis of the crowd,—a quite useless jumping of Panurge's sheep into the water to their obvious destruction.

But, besides the consideration of advantage, there is also another cause which ought to urge every man who is free from hypnosis and who understands the significance of his acts to refuse to do military service. A man cannot help but wish that his life should not be a useless, aimless existence, but that it should be a service to God and men. Frequently a man lives his life, without finding an opportunity for this service. The call to take part in military service is that opportunity which presents itself to every man of our time. Every man, by refusing to take part personally in military service, either as a recruit or as a payer of taxes to the government, which uses these taxes for military matters, by this refusal in the most efficacious manner does a great service to God and men, because by this refusal he in the most efficacious manner contributes to the forward movement of humanity toward that better social structure, toward which humanity is striving and at which it must arrive.

But it is not only advantageous to refuse to take part in military service, and not only ought this to be done,—for the majority of the men of our time, if they are at all free from hypnosis, it is impossible not to renounce military service. For every man there are certain acts which are morally impossible, just as impossible as are certain physical acts. Such a morally impossible act for the vast majority of the men of our time, if one is at all free from hypnosis, is the promise of slavish obedience to strangers and immoral men, whose professed aim is to kill men. And so every man of our time not only will find it advantageous and necessary to refuse to take part in military service, but even impossible to refrain

from doing so, if he is at all free from the stultification of
hypnosis.

"But what will happen, when all men shall refuse to do
military service, and there shall be no bridle and no fear on
the evil ones, and the evil ones shall triumph, and there shall
be no defence against the savages,—against the yellow race,—
who will come and conquer us?"

I shall not speak of the fact that the evil men have tri-
umphed long ago and still continue to triumph, and, struggling
among themselves, have for a long time been ruling over the
Christians, so that there is no cause for fearing what has happened long ago; nor shall I speak of this, that the fear of wild
and of yellow men, whom we persistently irritate and teach
war, is a barren excuse, and that for the imaginary defence
against these wild and yellow men one-hundredth part of
those armies which Europe now maintains would suffice. I
shall not speak of all that, because the considerations as to
what may happen to the world at large from such or such an
act of ours cannot serve as a guidance for our acts and our
activity. Man has given to him a different guide, one that
is incontestable—the guide of his conscience, by following
which he knows beyond a doubt that he is doing what he
ought to do. And so all the considerations about the dangers
which confront the separate individual who refuses to do
military service, as also about this, what danger threatens the
world in consequence of such refusals,—all those are particles
of that vast and terrible deception in which Christian humanity is enmeshed, and which is carefully maintained by the governments, which live by this deception.

From a man's acting as his reason, his conscience, his God
commands him to act, nothing but the best can result, both
for him and for the world.

The men of our time complain of the evil current of life
in our Christian world. This cannot be otherwise, when in
our consciousness we have recognized not only the fundamental divine commandment, "Do not kill," which was pro-
claimed thousands of years ago, but also the law of the love,

and brotherhood of all men, and when, in spite of this, every man of our European world in reality renounces this fundamental divine law, which he recognizes, and at the command of a president, emperor, minister, a Nicholas, a William, puts on a fool's costume, takes up instruments of murder, and says, "I am ready,—I will strike down, ruin, and kill whomsoever you command me to."

What, then, can society be, which is composed of such men? It must be terrible, and, indeed, it is terrible.

Bethink yourselves, brothers! Do not listen to those rascals who from your childhood infect you with the devilish spirit of patriotism, which is contrary to goodness and truth, and which is needed only to deprive you of your property, and your freedom, and your human dignity; and do not listen to those cheats who preach war in the name of God, a cruel and revengeful God, invented by them, and in the name of the false Christianity, which they have corrupted, and still less to those new Sadducees who in the name of science and enlightenment, wishing for nothing but the continuation of the present order, gather at meetings, write books, and make speeches, promising to establish a good and peaceful life for men without their efforts. Do not believe them. Believe in nothing but your feeling, which tells you that you are not animals or slaves, but free men, who are responsible for your acts, and so are unable to be murderers, either by your own will, or by the will of managers who live by these murders. You need only stop and think, in order that you may see all the terror and madness of what you have been doing, and, having come to see it, may stop doing the evil which you yourselves hate and which ruins you. And if you stop doing the evil, which you yourselves hate, there will naturally, without your effort, like owls before daylight, disappear all those ruling cheats, who at first corrupt you and then torment you, and there will naturally be formed those new human fraternal conditions of life, for which Christian humanity, worn out from suffering, exhausted from deception, and stuck fast in insolvable contradictions, has been yearning.

Let each man without any finely spun and complicated considerations and assumptions fulfil what his conscience indubitably tells him in our time, and he will know the justice of the Gospel words, "If any man will do His will, he shall know of the doctrine, whether it be of God, or whether I speak of myself" (John vii. 17).

April 23, 1898.

LETTER TO ERNEST HOWARD CROSBY

ON NON-RESISTANCE

(1896)

MY DEAR CROSBY:—I am very glad to hear of your activity and that it is beginning to attract attention. Fifty years ago Garrison's proclamation of non-resistance only cooled people toward him, and the whole fifty years' activity of Ballou in this direction was met with stubborn silence. I read with great pleasure in *Peace* the beautiful ideas of the American authors in regard to non-resistance. I make an exception only in the case of Mr. Bemis's old, unfounded opinion, which calumniates Christ in assuming that Christ's expulsion of the cattle from the temple means that he struck the men with a whip, and commanded his disciples to do likewise.

The ideas expressed by these writers, especially by H. Newton and G. Herron, are beautiful, but it is to be regretted that they do not answer the question which Christ put before men, but answer the question which the so-called orthodox teachers of the churches, the chief and most dangerous enemies of Christianity, have put in its place.

Mr. Higginson says that the law of non-resistance is not admissible as a general rule. H. Newton says that the practical results of the application of Christ's teaching will depend on the degree of faith which men will have in this teaching. Mr. C. Martyn assumes that the stage at which we are is not yet suited for the application of the teaching about non-resistance. G. Herron says that in order to fulfil the law of non-resistance, it is necessary to learn to apply it to

life. Mrs. Livermore says the same, thinking that the fulfilment of the law of non-resistance is possible only in the future.

All these opinions treat only the question as to what would
happen to people if all were put to the necessity of fulfilling
the law of non-resistance; but, in the first place, it is quite
impossible to compel all men to accept the law of non-resistance, and, in the second, if this were possible, it would be a
most glaring negation of the very principle which is being
established. To compel all men not to practise violence against
others! Who is going to compel men?

In the third place, and above all else, the question, as put
by Christ, does not consist in this, whether non-resistance
may become a universal law for all humanity, but what each
man must do in order to fulfil his destiny, to save his soul,
and do God's work, which reduces itself to the same.

The Christian teaching does not prescribe any laws for all
men; it does not say, "Follow such and such rules under fear
of punishment, and you will all be happy," but explains to
each separate man his position in the world and shows him
what for him personally results from this position. The
Christian teaching says to each individual man that his life,
if he recognizes his life to be his, and its aims, the worldly
good of his personality or of the personalities of other men,
can have no rational meaning, because this good, posited as
the end of life, can never be attained, because, in the first
place, all beings strive after the goods of the worldly life,
and these goods are always attained by one set of beings to
the detriment of others, so that every separate man cannot
receive the desired good, but, in all probability, must even
endure many unnecessary sufferings in his struggle for these
unattained goods; in the second place, because if a man even
attains the worldly goods, these, the more of them he attains,
satisfy him less and less, and he wishes for more and more
new ones; in the third place, mainly because the longer a
man lives, the more inevitably do old age, diseases, and finally
death, which destroys the possibility of any worldly good,
come to him.

Thus, if a man considers his life to be his, and its end to be the worldly good, for himself or for other men, this life can have for him no rational meaning. Life receives a rational meaning only when a man understands that the recognition of his life as his own, and the good of personality, of his own or of that of others, as its end, is an error, and that the human life does not belong to him, who has received this life from some one, but to Him who produced this life, and so its end must not consist in the attainment of his own good or of the good of others, but only in the fulfilment of the will of Him who produced it. Only with such a comprehension of life does it receive a rational meaning, and its end, which consists in the fulfilment of God's will, become attainable, and, above all, only with such a comprehension does man's activity become clearly defined, and he no longer is subject to despair and suffering, which were inevitable with his former comprehension.

"The world and I in it," such a man says to himself, "exist by the will of God. I cannot know the whole world and my relation to it, but I can know what is wanted of me by God, who sent men into this world, endless in time and space, and therefore inaccessible to my understanding, because this is revealed to me in the tradition, that is, in the aggregate reason of the best people in the world, who lived before me, and in my reason, and in my heart, that is, in the striving of my whole being.

"In the tradition, the aggregate of the wisdom of all the best men, who lived before me, I am told that I must act toward others as I wish that others should act toward me; my reason tells me that the greatest good of men is possible only when all men will act likewise.

"My heart is at peace and joyful only when I abandon myself to the feeling of love for men, which demands the same. And then I can not only know what I must do, but also the cause for which my activity is necessary and defined.

"I cannot grasp the whole divine work, for which the world exists and lives, but the divine work which is being accomplished in this world and in which I am taking part with my life is accessible to me. This work is the destruction of the discord and of the struggle among men and other beings, and the establishment among men of the greatest union, concord and love; this work is the realization of what the Jewish prophets promised, saying that the time will come when all men shall be taught the truth, when the spears shall be forged into pruning hooks, and the scythes and swords into plough-shares, and when the lion shall lie with the lamb."

Thus the man of the Christian comprehension of life not only knows how he must act in life, but also what he must do.

He must do what contributes to the establishment of the kingdom of God in the world. To do this, a man must fulfil the inner demands of God's will, that is, he must act amicably toward others, as he would like others to do to him. Thus the inner demands of a man's soul coincide with that external end of life which is placed before him.

And here though we have an indication which is so clear to a man of the Christian comprehension, and incontestable from two sides, as to what the meaning and end of human life consists in, and how a man must act, and what he must do, and what not, there appear certain people, who call themselves Christians, who decide that in such and such cases a man must depart from God's law and the common cause of life, which are given to him, and must act contrary to the law and the common cause of life, because, according to their ratiocination, the consequences of the acts committed according to God's law may be profitless and disadvantageous for men.

Man, according to the Christian teaching, is God's workman. The workman does not know his master's whole business, but the nearest aim to be attained by his work is revealed to him, and he is given definite indications as to what he should do; especially definite are the indications as to what he must not do, in order that he may not work against the aim for the attainment of which he was sent to work. In everything else he is given complete liberty. And so for a man who has grasped the Christian conception of life the meaning of his life is clear and rational, and he cannot have a moment of wavering as to how he should act in life and what he ought to do, in order to fulfil the destiny of his life.

According to the law given him in the tradition, in his reason, and in his heart, a man must always act toward another as he wishes to have done to him: he must contribute to the establishment of love and union among men; but according to the decision of these far-sighted people, a man must, while the fulfilment of the law, according to their opinion, is still premature, do violence, deprive of liberty, kill people, and with this contribute, not to union of love, but to the irritation and enragement of people. It is as though a mason, who is put to do certain definite work, who knows that he is taking part with others in the building of a house, and who has received a clear and indubitable command from the master himself that he is to lay a wall, should receive the command from other masons like him, who, like him, do not know the general plan of the structure and what is useful for the common work, to stop laying the wall, and to undo the work of the others.

Wonderful delusion! The being that breathes to-day and disappears to-morrow, that has one definite, incontestable law given to him, as to how he is to pass his short term of life, imagines that he knows what is necessary and useful and appropriate for all men, for the whole world, for that world which moves without cessation, and goes on developing, and in the name of this usefulness, which is differently understood by each of them, he prescribes to himself and to others for a time to depart from the unquestionable law, which is given to him and to all men, and not to act toward all men as he wants others to act toward him, not to bring love into the world, but to practise violence, to deprive of freedom, to punish, to kill, to introduce malice into the world, when it is found that this is necessary. And he enjoins us to do so knowing that the most terrible cruelties, tortures, murders of men, from the Inquisitions and punishments and terrors of all the revolutions to the present bestialities of the anarchists and the massacres of them, have all proceeded from this, that men suppose that they know what people and the world need; knowing that at any given moment there are always two opposite parties, each of which asserts that it is necessary to use violence against the opposite party,—the men of state against the anarchists, the anarchists against the men of state; the English against the Americans, the Americans against the English; the English against the Germans; and so forth, in all possible combinations and permutations.

Not only does a man of the Christian concept of life see clearly by reflection that there is no ground whatever for his departure from the law of his life, as clearly indicated to him by God, in order to follow the accidental, frail, frequently contradictory demands of men; but if he has been living the Christian life for some time, and has developed in himself the Christian moral sensitiveness, he can positively not act as people demand that he shall, not only as the result of reflection, but also of feeling.

As it is for many men of our world impossible to subject a child to torture and to kill it, though such a torture may save a hundred other people, so a whole series of acts becomes impossible for a man who has developed the Christian sensitiveness of his heart in himself. A Christian, for example, who is compelled to take part in court proceedings, where a man may be sentenced to capital punishment, to take part in matters of forcible seizure of other people's property, in discussions about the declaration of war, or in preparations for the same, to say nothing of war itself, finds himself in the same position in which a good man would be, if he were compelled to torture or kill a child. It is not that he decides by reflection what he ought not to do, but that he cannot do what is demanded of him, because for a man there exists the moral impossibility, just as there is a physical impossibility, of committing certain acts. Just as it is impossible for a man to lift up a mountain, as it is impossible for a good man to kill a child, so it is impossible for a man who lives a Christian life to take part in violence. Of what significance for such a man can be the reflections that for some imaginary good he must do what has become morally impossible for him?

How, then, is a man to act when he sees the obvious harm of following the law of love and the law of non-resistance, which results from it? How is a man to act—this example is always adduced—when a robber in his sight kills or injures a child, and when the child cannot be saved otherwise than by killing the robber?

It is generally assumed that, when they adduce such an example, there can be no other answer to the question than that the robber ought to be killed, in order that the child be saved. But this answer is given so emphatically and so quickly only because we are not only in the habit of acting in this manner in the case of the defence of a child, but also in the case of the expansion of the borders of a neighbouring state to the detriment of our own, or in the case of the transportation of lace across the border, or even in the case of the defence of the fruits of our garden against depredations by passers-by.

It is assumed that it is necessary to kill the robber in order to save the child, but we need only stop and think on what ground a man should act thus, be he a Christian or a non-Christian, to convince ourselves that such an act can have no rational foundations, and is considered necessary only because two thousand years ago such a mode of action was considered just and people were in the habit of acting thus. Why should a non-Christian, who does not recognize God and the meaning of life in the fulfilment of His will, kill the robber, in defending the child? To say nothing of this, that in killing the robber he is certainly killing, but does not know for certain until the very last moment whether the robber will kill the child or not, to say nothing of this irregularity: who has decided that the life of the child is more necessary and better than the life of the robber?

If a non-Christian does not recognize God, and does not consider the meaning of life to consist in the fulfilment of God's will, it is only calculation, that is, the consideration as to what is more profitable for him and for all men, the continuation of the robber's life or that of the child, which guides the choice of his acts. But to decide this, he must know what will become of the child which he saves, and what would become of the robber if he did not kill him. But that he cannot know. And so, if he is a non-Christian, he has no rational foundation for saving the child through the death of the robber.

But if a man is a Christian, and so recognizes God and sees the meaning of life in the fulfilment of His will, no matter what terrible robber may attack any innocent and beautiful child, he has still less cause to depart from the law given him by God and to do to the robber what the robber wants to do to the child; he may implore the robber, may place his body between the robber and his victim, but there is one thing he cannot do,—he cannot consciously depart from the law of God, the fulfilment of which forms the meaning of his life. It is very likely that, as the result of his bad bringing up and of his animality, a man, being a pagan or a Christian, will kill the robber, not only in the defence of the child, but also in his own defence or in the defence of his purse, but that will by no means signify that it is right to do so, that it is right to accustom ourselves and others to think that that ought to be done.

This will only mean that, in spite of the external education and Christianity, the habits of the stone age are still strong in man, that he is capable of committing acts which have long ago been disavowed by his consciousness. A robber in my sight is about to kill a child and I can save it by killing the robber; consequently it is necessary under certain conditions to resist evil with violence.

A man is in danger of his life and can be saved only through my lie; consequently it is necessary in certain cases to lie. A man is starving, and I cannot save him otherwise than by stealing; consequently it is necessary in certain cases to steal.

I lately read a story by Coppée, in which an orderly kills his officer, who has his life insured, and thus saves his honour and the life of his family. Consequently in certain cases it is right to kill.

Such imaginary cases and the conclusions drawn from them prove only this, that there are men who know that it is not right to lie, to kill, but who are so loath to stop doing this that they use all the efforts of their mind in order to justify their acts. There does not exist a moral rule for which it would be impossible to invent a situation when it would be hard to decide which is more moral, the departure from the rule or its fulfilment. The same is true of the question of non-resistance to evil: men know that it is bad, but they are so anxious to live by violence, that they use all the efforts of their mind, not for the elucidation of all the evil which is produced by man's recognition of the right to do violence to others, but for the defence of this right. But such invented cases in no way prove that the rules about not lying, stealing, killing are incorrect.

"*Fais ce que doit, advienne que pourra*,—do what is right, and let come what may,"—is an expression of profound wisdom. Each of us knows unquestionably what he ought to do, but none of us knows or can know what will happen. Thus we are brought to the same, not only by this, that we must do what is right, but also by this, that we know what is right, and do not know at all what will come and result from our acts.

The Christian teaching is a teaching as to what a man must do for the fulfilment of the will of Him who sent him into the world. But the reflections as to what consequences we assume to result from such or such acts of men not only have nothing in common with Christianity, but are that very delusion which destroys Christianity.

No one has yet seen the imaginary robber with the imaginary child, and all the horrors, which fill history and contemporary events, have been produced only because men imagine that they can know the consequences of the possible acts.

How is this? Men used to live a beastly life, violating

and killing all those whom it was advantageous for them to violate and kill, and even eating one another, thinking that that was right. Then there came a time, when, thousands of years ago, even in the time of Moses, there appeared the consciousness in men that it was bad to violate and kill one another. But there were some men for whom violence was advantageous, and they did not recognize the fact, and assured themselves and others that it was not always bad to violate and kill men, but that there were cases when this was necessary, useful, and even good. And acts of violence and murder, though not as frequent and cruel, were continued, but with this difference, that those who committed them justified them on the ground of usefulness to men. It was this false justification of violence that Christ arraigned. He showed that, since every act of violence could be justified, as actually happens, when two enemies do violence to one another and both consider their violence justifiable, and there is no chance of verifying the justice of the determination of either, it is necessary not to believe in any justifications of violence, and under no condition, as at first was thought right by humanity, is it necessary to make use of them.

It would seem that men who profess Christianity would have carefully to unveil this deception, because in the unveiling of this deception does one of the chief manifestations of Christianity consist. But the very opposite has happened: men to whom violence was advantageous, and who did not want to give up these advantages, took upon themselves the exclusive propaganda of Christianity, and, preaching it, asserted that, since there are cases in which the non-application of violence produces more evil than its application (the imaginary robber who kills the child), we must not fully accept Christ's teaching about non-resistance to evil, and that we may depart from this teaching in the defence of our lives and of those of other men, in the defence of our country, the protection of society from madmen and malefactors, and in many other cases. But the decision of the question as to when Christ's teaching ought to be set aside was left to those very men who made use of violence. Thus Christ's teaching about non-resistance to evil turned out to be absolutely set aside, and, what is worse than all that, those very men whom Christ arraigned began to consider themselves the exclusive preachers and expounders of His teachings. But the light shineth in the dark, and the false preachers of Christianity are again arraigned by His teaching.

We can think of the structure of the world as we please, we may do what is advantageous and agreeable for us to do, and use violence against people under the pretext of doing good to men, but it is absolutely impossible to assert that, in doing so, we are professing Christ's teaching, because Christ arraigned that very deception. The truth will sooner or later be made manifest, and will arraign the deceivers, even as it does now.

Let only the question of the human life be put correctly, as it was put by Christ and not as it was corrupted by the churches, and all the deceptions which by the churches have been heaped on Christ's teaching will fall of their own accord.

The question is not whether it will be good or bad for human society to follow the law of love and the resulting law of non-resistance, but whether you—a being that lives to-day and is dying by degrees to-morrow and every moment—will now, this very minute, fully do the will of Him who sent you and clearly expressed it in tradition and in your reason and heart, or whether you want to act contrary to this will. As soon as the question is put in this form, there will be but one answer: I want at once, this very minute, without any delay, without waiting for any one, and without considering the seeming consequences, with all my strength to fulfil what alone I am indubitably commanded to do by Him who sent me into the world, and in no case, under no condition, will I, can I, do what is contrary to it, because in this lies the only possibility of my rational, unwretched life.

January 12, 1896.

NOTE

Ernest Howard Crosby (1856-1907) American author,
lecturer and worker for civic reform,—member of the New
York legislature for four years and judge (by nomination of
President Harrison) of the mixed tribunal at Alexandria,
Egypt, for five years. Becoming dissatisfied with the results
of the political and judicial activity in which he had partici-
pated, he returned to the United States in 1894, and devoted
his time and energies to extra-governmental reforms. He was
an ardent advocate of international peace and an energetic
worker for single tax reform. His purpose during his later
years was to bring his life into conformity with the ideals of
Tolstoi and to transplant those ideals to America.

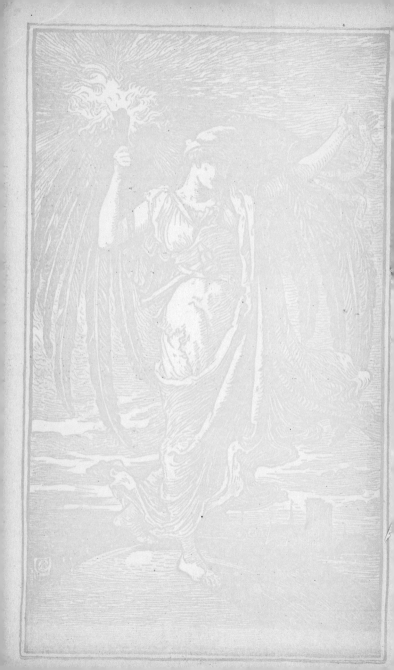